# GOD'S RADICAL PLAN
# FOR MARRIAGE

### Gil & Dana Stieglitz
With Jennifer Edwards

i

*God's Radical Plan for Wives*

Published by Principles to Live By, Roseville CA 95661
www.ptlb.com

Cover by John Chase
Copyedited by Jennifer Edwards, Sandy Johnson

All Scripture verses are from the New American Standard Bible unless otherwise indicated. New American Standard Bible: 1995 update. 1995 La Habra, CA: The Lockman Foundation.

Due to the sensitive subject matter, names and other identifying information have been altered to protect the privacy of those whose stories and quotes are included in the book.

ISBN 978-0-9838602-0-4
Christian Living /Marriage

Printed in the United States of America

*This book is dedicated to
the thousands of godly wives
who have decided to build great marriages
by loving their husbands deeply.*

# Table of Contents

# Introduction

This book grew out of the marriage ministry that I (Gil) had been conducting with men in my church for about ten years. Men learned what they had to do to build a great marriage, and they stepped up as spiritual leaders in their homes. They began to truly meet the deepest needs of their wives and the results were dramatic. Many of them pulled their marriages back from the brink of separation and divorce and built new relationships of lasting harmony and love. It was an exciting ministry to be involved in.

I never gave any thought to developing a series of lectures for women because, frankly, I perceived change mostly needed to take place on the men's side of the equation. I also felt that I could talk to, teach, and train to that side of the equation with expertise and passion. But one Sunday, a group of thirty-five women approached me. It appeared that after ten years of seeing dramatic results in marriage after marriage, it was time to address the other side of the equation—the wives. These wonderful ladies expressed how grateful they were for the material and training I had been giving their husbands but now felt it was unfair that their husbands knew how to meet their deepest needs, while they didn't know how to reciprocate. They asked that I teach a class for wives on how to meet the deepest needs of a man and love him at a new level. I successfully resisted for a while, but they were persistent! Finally their demands were met. I reluctantly agreed to teach a class to help them become "godly wives," even though I still did not have any idea what I would say to them.

When thirty-five women insist that you teach them how to be godly wives, you agree and then study to see what God wants you to say to them. I sat down with my computer Bible program and found every place in the Scriptures where the word *wife* is used. I worked through every reference and condensed a list of twenty-five or so actions and qualities that God wants in a wife. This list then became the basis of an early course for teaching *The Godly Wife* class. After a number of revisions, I took these biblical ideas and turned them into an acrostic—R.A.D.I.C.A.L. From the time the book, *God's Radical Plan for Husbands* (formerly *Becoming a Godly Husband*), was produced there had been increasing pressure from both men and women for a companion volume. So, I recruited my wife to work with me in the development of the manuscript to give me insights that only she in her walk with God and role as a wife had. I did the writing, but she read every page, correcting and keeping me from saying what I shouldn't, or from things that were not helpful.

The qualities and exercises in this book will put you in a position to bring about the positive changes you are hoping for in your marriage. It will be exciting when you take what you learn and begin to love him deeply. You will undoubtedly begin to experience life and vibrancy in your marriage at a whole new level. The enjoyment and satisfaction of your marriage will astound you. How do you change your husband and your marriage? You love him in unique ways, ultimately guiding him into meeting your needs. The Bible says that if husbands or wives will love their spouses deeply, then there will be a response from their mate (1 Peter 3:1-7; Ephesians 5:25-31). In this book we will

2

examine the specific duties and responsibilities that one side of the marriage equation has to play: that of the R.A.D.I.C.A.L. wife.

## Marriage Takes Work

We get married to have someone meet certain needs that no one else can meet. In a sense, we are laying out a job description for wives in this book just as I laid out a job description for husbands in *God's Radical Plan for Husbands*. These are the things that you can do to make your marriage work, even if your spouse isn't doing his part. The reward for doing them well will be a marriage rich with dividends. If left to chance, or done poorly, then the marriage becomes a constant source of heartache and pain.

To love someone is to meet his needs. Certain needs are exposed in marriage that only your spouse can meet. When the other person in your marriage meets your needs, you feel a huge piece of your life is filled in. When you experience the diligent attention of another person to your deep spiritual, emotional, mental, and physical needs, it not only provides you with joy but also with energy to meet their needs and to accomplish the work you must do in other responsibilities of your life. We get married to supply a missing ingredient in our lives.

It is extremely hard to write this book and put down on paper the deepest needs of a man. These are the secrets to manipulating a man's heart and/or fulfilling some of his greatest desires in life. If this material were to be used in a selfish, manipulative way, it could very well be some of the most destructive material ever penned. In fact, history records the exploits of women who understood the power of this material and manipulated their men to give up fortunes, abdicate positions of power, kill, destroy their own families, steal, and so on. But if this material were to be used by a woman who wants God's glory, not to mention a rich and rewarding marriage, it will be a treasure trove out of which she can build a joyful, vibrant life.

Deep inside the most important and powerful men in the world lives a little boy with needs – needs that only his woman can meet. Some men go their whole lives searching for a woman who will be dedicated to meeting those needs. Some men use multiple women to try to meet them, while always hoping that one of the women will be enough to meet them all. The power of a woman to complete her husband is immense and often controls whether that man becomes all God intended him to be or not. It has often been said that behind every successful man is a woman moving him forward. This is so true. One day we will present all that we did to our Lord Jesus Christ for evaluation (2 Corinthians 5:10). Our marriage will be part of what we present; and if it's a good marriage, we will have much more to show. Great marriages can be powerful equippers that allow us to accomplish all we are supposed to for God.

Too often men and women take a more selfish track and become consumed with whether their spouse is meeting their own needs or not. Wives can become self-absorbed in what their husband is not doing and how he should behave, instead of using the power of love to meet his needs and gently guide him to meet hers. In reality, he will really only begin to minister to her deepest needs only as she fills him up and moves him to a level of success he could never achieve on his own. In a sense, she is motivating her husband to achieve, stretch, and grow in all areas of his life.

Many concepts in this book will seem difficult and even servile to many women. We're quite certain there will even be some pushback at some of what is presented in this book. Hopefully, however, you will begin to realize that you have an opportunity to build the marriage of your dreams by enriching the lives of your husband in ways that even your husband did not think was possible. The point is this: a woman is not powerless to make changes in her marriage in a way that is both God-honoring and results-oriented. Scripture tells us something that is very hard to believe. In fact, most of us just quietly reject what it clearly states. In 1 Peter 3:1-2, we are told that if a woman understands how to meet the deepest needs of her husband, she can change him into a caring, intimate, enjoyable person without even talking about what he is doing wrong. All of it takes work, though. But it will be worth all that you give it.

## Pathways to Marital Bliss

There are two paths to marital bliss:
1. Your spouse meets your needs and makes you happy. You can't help but respond to his love. This is the preferred method for everyone, but it rarely happens this way. This is the "You change first" scenario.
2. Learn your spouse's deepest needs and begin to love him there. When you fill your spouse with your love, you then gently guide him to meet your needs and grow a great marriage.

Often I find that many people do not realize that God has signed them up for this second plan while they are still waiting (none too patiently) for the first scenario to take place.

## The Top Needs of Wives—H.U.S.B.A.N.D.

Before we start detailing what a wife should do to meet the deepest needs of her husband, it is imperative to outline the things I believe God prescribes for a husband to do to become a godly husband. In this way, we can demonstrate that we are not just

5

putting the huge burden of marital health all on the woman's shoulders. In my book, *God's Radical Plan for Husbands,* I outline the top needs of a woman using the acrostic H.U.S.B.A.N.D.:

- Honor—A godly husband chooses his wife as his number one priority in life, respecting and valuing the woman she was created to be. A part of meeting this need is to eliminate dishonor, sarcasm, and criticism. He needs to praise his wife every day for who she is, what she has done, and her abiding value as a person.

- Understanding—A man must learn to live with his wife in an understanding way—her more sensitive nature, her individual personality and temperament differences, and background, along with her unique gifts as a woman.

- Security—A man needs to demonstrate security in at least four specific areas in the relationship—physically, emotionally, verbally, and financially.

- Building unity—A husband builds unity between himself and his wife by helping her identify the common enemy so it is not always him. He works to build into the family lots of shared experiences out of which bonding and connectedness can grow.

- Agreement—A husband must develop a system of coming to agreement with his wife that respects her feelings, thoughts, and opinions as well as his own.

- Nurture—A godly husband looks after his wife's spiritual, mental, emotional, and physical needs, allowing her to reach her full potential. He considers her needs for communication, tenderness, romance, and leadership.

- **Defender**—A woman needs a man who will defend her against the arrows, pressures, temptations, negative people, and burdens of life.

## The Top Needs of Husbands—R.A.D.I.C.A.L.

In this book, we want to outline the practical steps of action that a wife can take to meet her husband's deepest needs, thereby building a marriage of great joy. I realize that a great marriage requires both partners working on the marriage, but that begins with one of the spouses. If more husbands and wives would stop complaining about their spouses and instead get busy loving more deeply, then we would see less heartache. Since you are the one reading this book, you might as well go first! It would be extremely helpful if you could get your husband to read *God's Radical Plan for Husbands* at the same time. Things would move a lot quicker then. The book and audiobook are available at www.principlestoliveby.com.

We have chosen to use the acrostic R.A.D.I.C.A.L. to outline a husband's deepest needs because it is easier to remember. If you really do minister to the needs in your husband's life, you really would be a *radical* wife, especially in our day and age. What elements make up the godly wife?

- **Respect**—A woman must learn how to respect and admire her husband. This is by far his greatest need, and he will do almost anything to get it.
- **Adaptation**—A godly wife adapts her strengths to make up for the weak areas of her husband. By adapting to who he really is, she finds a way to work together for a healthy and productive marriage.

- Domestic leadership—A woman's leadership in the home adds a lot of value to a man's world and is one of the key treasures that ties him to home and family.
- Intimacy—A godly wife seeks to meet her husband's needs for physical, emotional, spiritual, and mental intimacy.
- Companionship—A man is desperate for his wife to be his companion and partner. A godly wife recognizes that the key to a man's soul is by joining him in his hobby, work, or passion.
- Attractive soul and body—A woman who balances physical beauty and develops a beautiful soul keeps him coming back for more.
- Listening—The hidden need in a man is for his wife to listen to him in the way he needs to be heard.

These words spell out the deepest needs in a man and why he was drawn to his wife in the first place. During dating and courtship, at least for some period of time, she was meeting these needs or at least indicated that she would. He made a commitment to marry this woman based on the promise of her continuing to meet his needs.

## How to Use This Book

As you are about to dive into the details of being a godly wife, it is important to say that it is not possible to work on all these areas at once. The seven areas discussed in this book are open to endless improvement. Some wives have tried to make changes in all seven areas at once. Some have put themselves under a giant guilt trip because they are not already perfect in these seven areas. Rest assured, by meeting his deepest needs, your love for your husband has the ability to grow over time. As you act differently toward him and meet his deepest relational needs, he will be drawn toward you. Each area touches a specific aspect of his being. Granted, some men would rank these needs in different orders, therefore, wives should focus on the ones that her husband needs the most. We know we have included more exercises and projects than a person can do the first time through these concepts. It is often best to pick one aspect or exercise under one of the seven needs and focus on that until significant change is seen.

This material is designed to be a repeating touchstone for the creation of more love within a marriage. Each time you process through this material, you will reach new levels of change and understanding. Realize that a marriage is a long-term relationship of meeting each other's needs, enjoying one another, and working through the issues of two separate people trying to become one. Pick out one specific change in each chapter to work on. Make that change noticeable to your husband and watch your marriage change. Do not try to do too much or feel bad because you are not perfectly meeting his needs at all times. It's a process that takes time—hopefully you'll have a full lifetime of practicing together.

# Chapter 1

# The Wife Role

Women may assume many roles in their life: leader, employer, Christian, mother, volunteer, politician, and so on. One role that many women choose to embrace is wife but becoming a wife is more than just getting married. God says that to take on the role of wife is to be in a position of immense power (1 Peter 3:1-6). She has the power to change people in positive directions, starting with her husband and radiating out through her children and into the community. We realize that the role of wife has been diminished in the past because of the suggestion that wife and mother are the only two roles women can play. Our hope is that the true power of the wife role will re-emerge as the force God intended. We want to show you how to use the power of this role for God's glory, for the success of your husband, for the development of your marriage, and for meeting your deepest relational needs. God does have a RADICAL plan for wives. It is so transformative we would not have believed it if we hadn't seen it in the pages of Scripture and watched it work in real life.

## Historical View of Wives

For numerous millennia – before the modern, industrialized world – the wife role has been the foundation of every civilization and the most consistent means to harness masculinity for the common good. A wife is most likely the relational expert in the marriage. She can choose to be selfish or she can choose to be wise. She can really love her husband for God's glory, his benefit, and her deep satisfaction or she can selfishly demand that her needs and desires be met first, which will leave everyone bankrupt.

The current view of the magnificent role of a wife has been narrowed in scope since the industrial revolution. It is likened to a pretty bird in a gilded cage. The industrial revolution separated a man from his business and his business partner. His family was his business. His wife was his business partner. Each had a role to play in their economic, spiritual, mental, physical, and emotional survival. Understand that every family in the pre-modern world was a business that required both husbands and wives to contribute everything they had to survive and thrive. Realize that our world is going back to the pre-modern conditions of a family as an economic unit. It takes everyone in the family to survive and thrive these days. Yes, there are a few individuals who earn so much they are capable of sustaining the family on just their income, but that is the exception and not the norm. This new reality allows the role of a wife to be released from the prison of the Victorian mindset where a wife could only be involved in child rearing and charity work.

God actually wrote one of the most robust descriptions of the full-blown wife role through the pen of Solomon over 3,000 years ago. This description has baffled modern Christians because it does not fit the "gilded cage" understanding. God describes the dynamic wife in her full glory as a leader and lover, a shaper of the

12

community, her family, and her husband. In this example, the full power of her role is on display, blessing everyone. This is God's radical plan for wives. This passage may be familiar to you.

*"An excellent wife, who can find? For her worth is far above jewels. The heart of her husband trusts in her, and he will have no lack of gain. She does him good and not evil all the days of her life. She looks for wool and flax and works with her hands in delight. She is like merchant ships; she brings her food from afar. She rises also while it is still night and gives food to her household and portions to her maidens. She considers a field and buys it; from her earnings she plants a vineyard. She girds herself with strength and makes her arms strong. She senses that her gain is good; her lamp does not go out at night. She stretches out her hands to the distaff, and her hands grasp the spindle. She extends her hand to the poor, and she stretches out her hands to the needy. She is not afraid of the snow for her household, for all her household are clothed with scarlet. She makes coverings for herself; her clothing is fine linen and purple. Her husband is known in the gates, when he sits among the elders of the land. She makes linen garments and sells them, and supplies belts to the tradesmen. Strength and dignity are her clothing, and she smiles at the future. She opens her mouth in wisdom, and the teaching of kindness is on her tongue. She looks well to the ways of her household, and does not eat the bread of idleness. Her children rise up and bless her; her husband also, and he praises her, saying: "Many daughters have done nobly, but you excel them all." Charm is deceitful and beauty is vain, but a woman who fears the LORD, she shall be praised. Give her the product of her hands, and let her works praise her in the gates (Proverbs 31:10-31, NASB).*

13

This section of proverbs actually shows many of the radical aspects of the wife role we will discuss in this book:

- Deep respect and admiration she has for her husband
- Adaptation to the strengths and weakness of the husband's person and leadership
- Significant development of the domestic leadership component in the roles as business leader, mother, employer, planner, strategic thinker
- The growing development of an attractive soul and body
- The use of deep listening skills that draws the trust and praise of her husband

To throw oneself into the role of wife is no different than investing to become a great teacher, corporate executive, lawyer, or money manager. Each role has rules and strategies for maximizing the outcomes of that relationship. Becoming a wife means understanding the rules and strategies that maximize the relationship to everyone's benefit: the woman's, the man's, the children's, the community's, and so on. This is different from just being a married woman.

Though you may find yourself struggling with some of what you read, understand that we come to you humbly, presenting what the word of God says about the wonderful things a woman can do if she embraces her role as wife. It is time to examine the real secrets of the wife role. It is powerful and makes a marked difference in people's lives and marriages. We wouldn't have believed it could work if we hadn't seen it with our own eyes. Let us say again that a wife's role is not the only role a woman can play. It is one of many roles she can play if she is married.

As we examine the various aspects of the role throughout this book, you may recognize women, girlfriends, and wives who have excelled at pieces of the wife role. What will happen if a woman has the whole playbook and knows when to use its various secrets? She'll fulfill this role with excellence. She'll develop a great life for herself, her husband, her children, and her community. Every wife that embraces God's radical plan for her role deserves honor and praise. Kudos to her! Let's look at the whole.

# Chapter 2

## Affecting Change

One of the goals of this book is to be able to more clearly understand your husband and what motivates him. Let me start off by saying that every husband has deep relational needs that can only righteously be met in his marriage. If he is going to maximize his roles of husband, father, Christian, leader, and employer/employee, then specific relational needs must be met in the relationship he has with his wife. He was willing to marry you because he felt you were meeting some of his deepest relational needs at some point.

Certainly women also have deep relational needs that only he can meet, but those needs are completely different than his needs. Yes, he should meet them. But how can he if he doesn't know or understand what they are? If you learn how to embrace the full wife role, you will be able to teach him what your needs are and how to meet them. Believe it or not, they are not intuitive to a man. He has to be led and guided. This is where you come in.

If a married woman understands what her husband's relational needs are and begins to meet them consistently, she begins to become a "wife" in the truest sense of the word. She begins to fulfill 1 Peter 3:1-6 and maximize her husband's potential for everybody's benefit. A working biblical definition of love is to meet needs, pursue, and please. Love is an action, not a feeling. If someone has a need and I meet that need, then I have loved them whether I feel anything towards them or not. In most cases, the person who has the feeling is the person who has been loved, not the lover.

I am going to suggest that what God is saying to wives is that they become lovers of their husbands at a whole new level, thereby motivating their husbands to follow God in becoming the best version of themselves they can be. By doing this, they will then be able to meet their wife's deep relational needs. To get your husband to the point of being able to meet your needs, I would like to introduce to you a concept called, "The Dolphin Experiment."

What I am going to say about dolphin training is somewhat controversial, and there is not a one-to-one correlation between the metaphor of dolphins and your husband. But there is much to learn about motivation. When animal trainers begin training dolphins to jump high in the air, go over a rope, or do flips, they start in a very basic way. The trainer puts a rope near the bottom of the pool where the dolphin is swimming. Every time the dolphin swims over the rope, it gets a fish when it comes to the surface. Every time the dolphin swims under the rope, it gets no fish.

At first the receiving of fish seems completely random to the dolphin. The dolphin does not know our language and cannot understand what the trainer wants. It doesn't comprehend why the trainer would want him to do certain things. It has made no connection. The dolphin is just "grateful" for the fish that comes at random intervals. At some point – maybe a week or two later – the trainer puts the rope in the middle of the tank where the dolphin has a 50/50 chance of swimming over the rope or under

18

the rope. If it goes over, then it gets a fish. If it goes under, then it receives nothing. Slowly, but surely, the dolphin begins to realize that "over the rope" means fish.

After a few weeks, the trainer puts the rope about a foot from the surface. It is now unlikely that the dolphin will randomly swim over the rope. But still, every time the dolphin swims over the rope, it gets a fish; and every time it swims under the rope, it receives nothing. The trainer is cementing in the dolphin's mind that "over" means "reward." After a week or so the rope is put on the surface of the water. If the dolphin consistently goes over the rope and gets the fish, then the trainer knows that the concept is locked in and they can raise the rope as high as they want—the dolphin will go over the rope. It wants the fish and it fully understands the connection between the rope and the fish. It's quite amazing actually!

## Learning a New Language

Like the dolphin and the trainer, your husband does not speak your language. It is difficult for him to understand why you do what you do sometimes and not other times. He is anxiously trying to find a pattern as to when he can expect his relational needs to be met. He does not make the connections that you are making. He thinks things like,

- "When I brought home flowers (or took her on a date), we had sex. I'll do that every other day."

- "When I emptied the dishwasher, she was in a good mood and didn't nag me. I will do that every night first thing."

What he doesn't realize is that you need him to put you first even above himself; to understand your personality, moods, dreams, and abilities; to build your sense of security through sound financial management; to be calm in the face of stress; to focus on your beauty, not other women; and so on. He believes that you both want the same things out of the marriage that he does, so he does not understand why you don't consistently want to do what he finds so enjoyable. He needs to know what you need, and he wants it spelled out to him in a way he understands. Remember, he does not speak your language, and he does not have the same internal needs you do. In many ways he is looking for a direct linear connection between what he does and what you do for him. Now obviously we are oversimplifying this but understand that the feminine world is a mystery to him, and connections that direct his actions really help. He needs to know when he is doing a good job and when he is not. And when he does it right, he needs a fish.

## What Are His Fish?

Your deepest relational needs are as foreign to him as a dolphin swimming over a rope. He doesn't have any motivation to do that naturally. Instead, he is looking for his needs to be met. He is looking for what he is interested in—his "fish." His fish are the needs outlined in this book:

- Respect & Admiration
- Adaptation
- Domestic leadership in the home
- Intimacy & Sex
- Companionship
- A beautiful wife, both on the inside and out
- Listening in a therapeutic way

If you give him these "fish," and help him understand why he is receiving these "rewards," then he will be delighted with this marriage relationship. When you tie the meeting of your needs with the meeting of his needs, then you both win an incredible, loving marriage. This is an unemotional description of what it means to love him. He is hoping that you come to enjoy being with him, ministering to him, and having your needs met by him. Really, that is what you said to him when you pledged, "I do." You essentially communicated, "I want this man to meet my deepest relational needs, and I pledge myself to meet his deepest relational needs."

The above descriptions may seem like an extremely crass way of putting it, but I do believe it communicates the essential truth. Your husband needs you to meet his relational needs (give him a fish) and show him how to consistently meet your needs. The result is that everyone lives in harmony.

In most cases, a husband does not understand what his wife needs relationally and how much she would blossom if he were to consistently meet her deepest relational needs. He may not understand how much more successful he could be with a few changes. Or the difference he can make in the lives of the children with just a few hours of involvement. In many cases, he does not comprehend the way to become a respectable and prominent member of the community. Or how much adding more of God in his life would strap rockets to his life. In other words, he needs you to show him these things in order to experience these positive outcomes.

I know a number of married women who object to playing the wife role because it feels demeaning. Unfortunately these women suffer for their refusal to do so—emotionally, financially, mentally, spiritually, and even sometimes physically. They never achieve the full potential of joy in their marriage because they steadfastly cling to their independence and selfish point of view.

21

We hear it all the time, "Why isn't he meeting my needs? I deserve to be happy." "He should meet my needs first, because I am so special." "His needs are gross or weird; why doesn't he change?" The vital ingredients that come from that role are not injected into their husbands, so the marriage and family suffers for it. Just like a teacher must prepare lesson plans or a nurse or a lawyer must study and practice in order to do their role well, a wife must grow in the ability to do this role so that her husband and family can maximally benefit.

Realistically, it takes approximately one to four hours on any given day to fulfill the wife role exceptionally well. How do I know that it only takes one to four hours a day? Because that is the amount of time the average couple spends together when dating—when they are selling each other on the fact that they can meet each other's relational needs. It is also the usual amount of time that a husband and wife see each other on the average day. Don't you think a few hours of your time is worth the investment to live in a marriage that is a delight to both you and your husband? Invest time to develop skills to do this "job" to the best of your ability. It is a cultivated skill and there are rewards for those who learn them—great relationships and a great environment to live in.

## A Role that Benefits Everyone

To give you an idea of how playing a role in a particular relationship benefits everyone, let's look at the monetary and business arenas. Making money and building financial security involves certain rules. If you follow them, you will receive more money or retain what you already receive. If you violate them, you will let what does come to you slip through your fingers. It is not demeaning to learn those rules and use them to build financial security.

In a similar vein, I know a number of people who work at various companies, but they do not really work as hard or to the best of their ability to make sure the company strongly benefits from their involvement. These people are always shocked when they do not get promoted or receive raises, and they are usually the first to be let go when a downturn takes place. It is not demeaning to learn the rules of being a hardworking employee in order to benefit the company they work for. And it is essential to get ahead at that company.

Every successful employer or employee comes to work with a cooperative attitude. How do I contribute to this company in a positive way? How do I encourage my boss, my colleagues, and my subordinates? How do I win personally through the tasks, functions, and confines of my present job? Successful employers and employees don't say, "How do I get everybody else to do what I want?" They have a primary concern about the health of the organization. They ask, "What will bring about a healthy organization?"

A marriage is an organization, too. Both a man and a woman contribute to the health of that organization. A wife does her part when she takes on the full role of wife. If instead she says, "I am just going to sit back and let my husband take care of me and minister to my needs," she puts the whole organization at risk. In the same way, if a husband says, "Now that I am married, I will do nothing to improve the health of our marriage and family or meet my wife's needs," he puts the whole marriage organization at risk. A marriage does not improve if one or both of the partners decides to be selfish.

Just like in the other examples, it is not demeaning to learn the rules of being a "wife" and then use them to build a great marriage. If she does that, she will be successful, and her husband and family will be successful – all for God's glory.

## How Does This Look?

To show you what this looks like in real life, we'll give you a few examples from our own marriage.

Dana says: "When our children were little, Gil wanted to help watch and care for them. He changed diapers and clothed them while I attended to other issues in our family and in the church. I noticed that he would regularly put the diapers on backwards or dress the girls in hideous outfits. My first temptation was to tell him that he had done it wrong or to make fun of his efforts. But I realized that if I wanted him to continue to pitch in, I needed to admire him for what he had done and display an unusual level of gratefulness for his attempts to help. Yes, the results were not always up to my 'standards,' but he was trying and it was helpful. I rewarded him for what he did and for the effort he made rather than withholding rewards until he did it perfectly.

Gil wants to do all he can for our family to succeed, but he rarely helps perfectly according to my standards, especially at first. If I had waited to reward him until he did things perfectly, he would have given up helping a long time ago. He keeps getting better and more helpful over time, and I keep encouraging him to help in every way I can.

It's funny, because when he empties the dishwasher, he probably expects 'husband of the year' honors for his sacrifice. He maybe puts the plates in the wrong places or doesn't put the silverware away like I would have, but I made it a habit to admire, be thankful, and appreciate him for all his attempts."

Gil says, "I think that's why I have come to enjoy helping in the kitchen—I like the rewards and I want more of them!"

# Chapter 3

## Respect

*Ephesians 5:33; Proverbs 12:4*

Beth was not a beauty by the world's standards, but her husband was completely enamored with her. Many people wondered how this plain woman held on to a man like Dave. After all, he was handsome, articulate, and successful. Many pegged him as a prime candidate for an affair, but he did not stray. Rather, he was completely entranced by his wife and to him she was beautiful in every way. Did he not realize how plain she really looked? Did she hold something dark over him that made him stay close to her? What did she do to hold her husband's affection so powerfully that he never considered being with another woman? What was her secret? Beth had a master key to the lost art of modern romance and marriage today. Indeed, more than any other person in his life, she made him feel valued through respect and admiration.

It is true that most women do not understand that men have an incredibly deep need to be respected and admired. If a woman can learn how to apply this biblical principle to her marriage, she will become a powerful magnet that attracts and holds her man's affection. Visualize with me for a moment a flower that turns its face toward the sun as it moves across the sky. Men are the same, in that they turn without fail toward a woman who respects him. Or like a moth that is irresistibly drawn towards the light. Respect and admiration from a woman draws a man's attention just like that light. A respected and admired husband will be loyal to the source of that energy, which hopefully radiates from his wife. By respecting and admiring her husband every day, she plays an important part in building a vibrant marriage of great joy.

## The Biblical Command

*However, each one of you also must love his wife as he loves himself, and the wife must respect her husband. Ephesians 5:33 (NIV)*

*A wife of noble character is her husband's crown, but a disgraceful wife is like decay in his bones. Proverbs 12:4 (NIV)*

The Scriptures are clear for both men and women even though sometimes we don't want to obey them. The Bible says in Ephesians 5:33 that husbands are to love their wives as themselves, but that wives *must see to it that she respects her husband.* Similarly, Proverbs 12:4 describes the excellent (godly) wife as being the crown of her husband, but she who shames him is like rottenness in his bones! I have found it to be true that God commands us to do the things that we would not naturally do. As I point out in my book, *God's Radical Plan for Husbands,* He specifically commands men to love their wives in the ways that meet her deepest needs. In the same way, God commands women to go outside of their comfort zone and meet the deepest need of their husband which, according to the Scriptures, is respect. Once they do, they will be able to build the kind of marriage that they long for.

## What Does Respect Mean?

A working definition of the word *respect* is *to acknowledge value*. It means to focus attention on a person's strengths, contributions, positions, accomplishments, and abilities. Many people believe that respect is something that has to be *earned*. To a certain degree this is true. But, more importantly, referencing the command in Ephesians 5:33, respect is to be given before it is earned. To respect a person is to act, speak, and refer to someone in terms of the valuable things in the person's life instead of the mistakes, problems, and weaknesses. It means to admire the person for who they are and the positive things they have done.

The Greek word translated as *respect* in Ephesians 5:33 is the word *phobetai*, which comes from the word *phobia* or *fear of*. This word means that the person or object is of such a high value that one would be afraid of devaluing them or not attributing them their proper value. The Apostle Paul wanted to make sure that women understand the absolute importance of valuing their husbands. God places great value on the husband and the role in the family. So likewise, wives should to. Her ability to do this on a consistent basis will help create a stable relationship and build intimacy in her marriage. On the other hand, if a wife focuses on his weaknesses, mistakes, and inabilities, she will destroy him along with the marriage.

## What Does Respect Do?

In its most basic sense, respect is like energy that fuels his efforts to attempt and achieve what he could not, or would not, accomplish on his own. Thus, a respected man is energized to do the things required to be successful in life and marriage; he is able to achieve his full, God-given potential and become the man God created him to be if he is respected. If a wife were to think back on

29

the dating phase of their relationship, she would begin to realize that she probably met this need in him at one point without even realizing it. She admired him, respected him, and doted on the things he did well. In fact, it can be safely said that no man marries a woman who cannot meet this need in him. The evidence that she met this need in him at one time is by the fact that they married. Certainly, no man would commit himself for life to a woman who had not demonstrated respect or showed him admiration during the relationship.

Evidence that this affirming treatment will continue in the future also weighs heavily in a man's decision to marry. It probably never occurs to him that his wife will start looking for a new list of things he needs to do to earn her respect once they are married. If he did, he would likely not commit to her. Like I said before, men are irresistibly drawn toward a woman who responds to him with respect and admiration. It simply satisfies a deep need – a craving if you will – to be valued and admired by her.

The tragedy of many marriages I have counseled starts when the wife begins to do the opposite of showing respect and admiration. I have seen cases when this happens as soon as the wedding is over! Over time, she begins to notice all the things he is doing wrong or not doing at all. The focus shifts away from his strengths and successes to his problems and weaknesses, which creates a negative attitude of disrespect within her. Before she was living with him 24/7, he could put his best foot forward and she likely overlooked all the signs of his seamier side. But after the wedding, when many men let their guard down, the hidden sides of his life become exposed.

Though she may have respected and admired him at one time, she now has a hard time because of all the flaws, weakness, and stupidity she sees in him. Disrespect oozes out through criticism or looks of shock, disappointment, and disapproval. Chiding becomes the norm as an attempt to stimulate him to greater action and productivity. Sadly, she doesn't realize that this behavior demeans him and does the very opposite of what she tries to do. He begins to withdraw from her along with his motivation to try; his energy to love her wanes and the wedding bliss is soured.

Now I realize that some of the sour attitude may come as a result of a husband not doing the things she asks. Maybe he isn't meeting a certain expectation or doesn't understand her priorities. I get that. Men can sometimes be pretty thick, and we are often one-tracked. What I am saying about this area of respect, however, is that a wife's diligence lays the groundwork to help him understand how to best meet her needs. Cutting off respect will never generate the results she is after. So, first we know that respect, approval, and admiration are powerful tools. We also know that if a man is in a relationship with a woman, he wants— no, needs desperately—those things from her. If he stops getting them, something deep within him begins to die.

The good news is that wives can reignite this powerful marriage-building tool. When she does, her relationship with her husband can flourish again. Without it, the marriage cannot be all that it was meant to be. So in order to save or strengthen her marriage, she must choose to focus once again upon the strengths, abilities, success, and efforts of her husband or else he will never become the dream spouse she is hoping he will be. Yes, it is possible for a woman to re-train herself to respect and admire him deeply. He really is like the kindergartener bringing home his finger paintings to his mom seeking her approval, "Did I do good?" He desperately needs to hear, "You did good! I'm proud of you."

What does respecting your husband look like? In simple terms, it means doing anything that you as a woman can do to acknowledge his value and worth. When a wife regularly appreciates the work he does, the skills he has, and the things he knows, this is acknowledging his value. It seems strange to state that a man needs to be validated by his wife, but God created men to have this unique need. Remember, he chose to be in a relationship with you because at some point you validated him as significant, important, and valuable. I realize that after living with him for a while, your opinion of who he is may have changed; but he still needs you to validate his worth. Think about his attributes, talents, abilities, and strengths.

*Does he smell nice?*
*Can he fix things?*
*Is he gifted in his career?*
*Can he do unique or special things?*

Whatever they are, find them and compliment him. There is more to come about that later in this chapter.

## Sources of Respect

Every person has a number of sources where they find respect. We often rely upon people, positions, and material things in our life to tell us we are valuable. It's just human nature. This issue of respect resides in every relationship and is usually heightened in those closest to us. In other words, we want those who know us best to have the highest opinions of us. We need these people to overlook our weaknesses and emphasize our strengths. Granted there is no *one* person who can completely fill you up in the area of respect, but there are crucial people who should supply high doses of respect and admiration. Tragically, when they don't supply this need, it creates a deep hole in our lives.

Parents, spouses, teachers, and children are a few of the most crucial people who should be a steady source of respect and value. Think about how devastating it is if the people who should be focused on your strengths, successes, and abilities instead put you down and constantly criticize and demean you. It is really a double blow. When the key people in your life acknowledge that you are valuable through listening, caring, spending money, giving time, encouraging, celebrating success, bestowing titles and positive nicknames, it acts as a powerful energy source for you to achieve your full potential.

Consider every act of respect you give your husband as a deposit into his emotional bank account. Every time you listen, care for him, give your time, encourage him, celebrate his successes, and love him intimately, it is like money in the bank. Now, if the balance in his account is high, he can handle a few withdrawals (things you need from him or things you have to say) without suffering too much. But if his balance is low, even the smallest of withdrawals can bankrupt him. By the way, this holds true for children, too.

Think this through: Do you have key people in your life that regularly let you know how valuable you are? Does your husband? Do your children? If the answer is yes, then all the energy is there to tackle the challenges in life. This applies even more for your husband.

## Dangers of A Need Not Met

There are several risks that wives take when they withhold respect from their husband. It's no secret that a man's desire to be respected and admired by a woman is so powerful that he will do

33

almost anything to satisfy it. Countless books have been written on the topic of respect and the power women have in this area. It seems like many wives wait for their husband to do something respectable before they begin to value them. Unfortunately, while they are waiting around for the impossible to happen, the need is still there—unmet. Since this is a need inherent in all men, it will be met somehow – only maybe not by her. Wives, if you do not initiate giving your husband respect, whether it is deserved or not, he will begin to search for importance and respect from others outside the home. He will keep searching until he finds people who value him and think he is important. This could be people at work, friends, other women, or anyone with similar interests.

We have all heard about men who agreed to lie, steal, cheat, move, leave family—even kill—to gain respect and admiration from his wife. The need for it is so strong that he will do whatever it takes to get more of it even if that means working more hours, buying expensive gifts, and so on. His usual solutions are to do more of what seemed to gain her respect in the past. But if nothing he tries works, he eventually stops trying. When this happens, he closes his heart to his wife, and the marriage becomes strictly a business relationship. He disengages emotionally, mentally, and physically, and will tend to move toward other sources of respect in his life. It is not uncommon for men to spend inordinate amounts of time with a hobby, at a lodge, or civic organization because he receives a feeling of respect, importance, and satisfaction that he doesn't receive at home. The sources from where he receives respect and significance will get more of his time, energy, and attention.

A man may elect to continue with the marriage out of duty – at least for a while – but he may also conclude that he needs to look elsewhere. Many men do. Indeed, the price of a lack of respect can be extremely costly. Affairs typically occur when a man encounters a woman who shows him the respect that he may not be receiving or feeling at home. This new woman gives him feelings of importance and value. If he doesn't feel valued at home, then there isn't a strong enough anchor to keep him from resisting the charms of this other woman. I have counseled hundreds of men who have committed extra-marital affairs on their wives. When asked why they did so, the common answer was that the mistresses made them feel special whenever they were together, like somebody valuable. "She admired me," they said. We have even seen throughout history the classic example of men becoming traitors to their own country because a beautiful woman seduced him with respect, admiration, and hero worship that he had never experienced before.

Usually a husband's participation in an extra-marital affair comes as an awful shock. The discovery is met with complete surprise and horror, followed by feelings of betrayal and great pain. Let's face it, no one ever believes their spouses could cheat on them but affairs happen all the time. The reverse can also be true. Wives can be tempted toward an extra-marital affair themselves when they only allow themselves to focus on the negative traits of their husbands (how he is not meeting her needs), rather than loving him for who he is. She may begin to see things in other men that her husband lacks which may or may not be true. I've seen it time and time again. Affairs can and do devastate marriages, homes, and lives.

Really no marriage is completely safe from infidelity. That's why I can't stress enough how important it is to do what you can to guard against it. Affair-proof your marriage by resolving to meet this need of respect in your husband.

There are other consequences to consider when this need is not met. Without respect, men are less motivated to achieve their full potential. In general, men are motivated to win a woman's approval. In order to do that, he will often reach beyond himself to gain it. If, however, it becomes clear to him that no matter what he does he will never measure up, he usually gives up and disengages from marriage and family life. The lack of respect robs him of the energy and motivation to change his habits and improve his station in life. Wives, if you want to bring about change in your husband that will allow him to become maximally successful, then begin a deliberate campaign of respecting him. Understand that big changes might not happen overnight—it takes time for these things—but you may notice small changes begin to surface. The more you display your affection, admiration, and respect for him, the more he will be drawn to you. He'll always come back for more. Meeting his desire for respect will help him become all the man you know he can be.

Men who don't receive respect develop wounds in their soul, leaving them with less joy and overflow to give to others. In fact, men in our culture often suffer through three deep wounds that leave them living a life of quiet desperation. First, the *father wound* is one in which a son is waiting for his father to announce how proud of him he is and his pleasure with how he turned out. Sadly, a huge unspoken heartache exists in men where fathers never expressed or demonstrated that they are proud of their sons. A father's blessing and respect fuel a powerful internal engine for men. A man who is unsure of his father's feelings for him is often emotionally crippled. Somewhere around 80 to 90 percent of the men in this culture are deeply wounded because there is no accepted cultural way for fathers to convey this needed acceptance to their sons.

36

A *mother wound* is another type of wound created by an unhealthy, emotional relationship with his mother which causes him to either be threatened by the influence of women later in life or to over-identify and become submissive to the influence of women. His perception of women – especially the role that his wife plays in marriage – becomes skewed. He may rely on her to fill an emotional need that she cannot fill on her own. Men with *mother wounds* tend to be either dominant or passive towards women. These wounds can occur if moms don't understand a boy's need to connect with other men. This is especially true for single moms who may overcompensate if their son is without male figures or mentors in their lives. It can also occur when a woman who has lost an emotional connection with her husband begins to transfer the connection over to her son. Men with *mother wounds* have described situations when their mother was unwilling to release him into adulthood, wanting to exert her control well beyond what was healthy. And still other men have come to realize that their moms were unable to care for them in the way children are meant to be cared for, due to her own emotional or physical issues, addictions, or a general absence in his life. As you can see, motherhood has a profound impact on the lives of children for the good or the bad.

The third wound is what we often call the *wife wound*. This wounding occurs when a man does everything he knows to do to provide for and please his wife and family, yet all he receives are requests for more—or criticisms of what he hasn't done right. When this is the case, it creates a rift and feelings of resentment and hopelessness set in. Husbands are waiting for their wives to demonstrate that they deeply respect and value him for all his work, sacrifice, and self-denial. Most men wait their entire life to hear that their wives respect them. It doesn't often show, but a man needs his wife to admire him and openly value his contribution, his person, his abilities, and his sacrifices. He needs to hear, "You've done good" every day—someone to "toot his horn" because he often won't toot his own. Sadly, it seems like the only culturally accepted way of conveying the level of respect he needs comes at his funeral after he is gone. He needs to see respect in your eyes *today*! To see it in the way you talk to him *now*, in what you give up to be with him, the way you speak about him, how you dress for him, your attitude towards him, and your interest in the things he values and likes to do. We'll cover more about those things in the chapters to come.

Without respect, the husband's worst fear is realized that they are made to feel like failures. Have you ever seen women demean their husbands in public? I can tell you it's a very uncomfortable situation. They think they are being clever, acting all in charge by revealing their husband's shortcomings. It's so hard to listen to! In reality, though, it's a clear indicator that their marriage is in trouble even if they don't know it yet. We can't stress enough how important it is to always speak well of your husband in front of others, especially other women.

Even if wives don't publically demean their husbands, men know when they aren't being respected—call it a sixth sense if you will. Men can tell if you harbor feelings of resentment and disrespect. Those feelings show up in how you treat him and the way you speak to him. He may not be aware of it consciously, but on the more subtle and subconscious level, he is aware that he means less to you than he used to. When a man is made to feel like a failure, he can easily overreact to his wife's requests because the only thing he hears is, "YOU ARE A FAILURE!" Even though this seems somewhat irrational, it's what happens when a man's "fear button of failure" is pressed. They may display emotional outbursts or give way to illogical argumentations—things he does to save face in front of you. But when a man feels valued, he can handle hearing some criticism, like things he could have done better or differently because he is not fighting for self-respect. He won't freak out or get too defensive because he knows it's not an attack on his manhood! Without this context of respect, however, it is hard for a man to receive correction. Remember the example we used of the emotional bank account? This is what we are talking about. If you can help him come to realize how much you value him as a man in your life and how valuable he is to the family, work, church, his friends, and the community, then you provide a context in which he can receive correction. Remember that your respect is what gives him the energy and desire to try harder and even to tackle your "to-do" list. With it he will want to grow in his sensitivity to you and be even more responsive to your requests since you are the person who gives him more respect than any other person in the world.

## Learning to Respect Him

When we trust God and obey what He tells us to do, we can rest in faith that He will take care of the outcome. When you step out and initiate change, everybody wins. You have the power to go first, even if you'd rather not. In this section we will show you eleven ways to renew or foster the respect that your husband genuinely needs and craves. The goal here is to remind you of his positive qualities and reignite respect for him. We recommend doing each of the marriage exercises provided below as they are designed to focus your attention on him as a man. Some of them take longer than others but take as much time as you need. They will help you to think through some of the things we are saying and organize your thoughts.

By the end, they will give you a new perception and perspective of your husband as a person and a man. We encourage you to spend some time thinking them through and writing down your answers in a journal. Every few years coming back to this list of exercises with a fresh sheet of paper will allow you to find new answers and new perspectives on your husband. They are designed to encourage you to take a more positive look at your husband and hopefully remind you about why you respected and admired him in the first place.

### Focus on what he does well.

A husband desperately needs a wife who will focus her attention on what he does right. All men have weaknesses and they usually know what they are. In fact, most are keenly aware of their shortcomings. Many women feel that they could have a fairly good husband if they just helped him to improve in a couple of the areas where he is deficient. With this in mind, many women then set out to begin a "husband-improvement campaign." Typically, this kind of effort is usually met with a great deal of resistance and even anger.

Let me assure you that your husband married you because he thought you accepted, respected, and loved him as he is now. He has a certain number of abilities, talents, strengths, and gifts with a huge need to be complimented, valued, and compensated for them. If he is going to make the changes necessary to achieve his greatest potential, it will be because the people closest to him energize him through respect and focus on his strengths. It is a truism in life. We gain strength to change when people accept us, respect what we do, and love us. It is also true that people rarely change when they feel unappreciated, forced, coerced, or manipulated to change.

Most wives know the areas that are holding their husbands back from being all they could be. If they choose to focus on changing those areas rather than what he does well, there is usually resistance. A man wants his wife to be his friend and friends focus on what they like about you, overlooking what they don't like. Typically in friendship, we do not remain friends with people who constantly point out our mistakes or mess-ups. We stop opening up to them and cease spending time with them. The same thing happens between husbands and wives.

Sometimes a wife decides that what she doesn't like about him is so glaring that she struggles to remember her husband's positive qualities. Keep in mind, though, that you are committed in Holy Matrimony with this man for life. It may be time to start digging for reasons to applaud him. Yes, there may be some things that drive you crazy about your husband, so the only way to see those changes take place is to give them to God and pray them out of his life. God is able to do exciting things when we surrender our control. It's exciting when change occurs, and you know that God accomplished them in your husband's life because you let go.

## Marriage Exercise #1

### What Does He Do Well?

1. Write down five specific things your husband does well.
   - 
   - 
   - 
   - 
   - 

2. Compliment him specifically about one of these strengths each day.

3. Write him a note, postcard, or email this week expressing appreciation for one of his specific abilities.

## Seek out his strengths.

God designed men to be strong, and he designed women to love strong men. We can find evidence of a man's strength in his life and marriage when we look at his experiences, abilities, accomplishments; what he refrains from or avoids; the ways God has gifted him spiritually; and his God-given personality temperament. Not all men are physically strong. Your husband may be extremely strong in character or integrity. He may have strength in a skill or ability that other men don't. Whatever it is, your husband is a strong man. Let these exercises remind you of his strengths.

### Marriage Exercise #2

### What Are His Strengths?

What are his obvious strengths? Be as specific as possible. Don't just write down that your husband is smart; rather, specify his intelligence: He knows a lot about politics, he knows how to run a profitable business, or he knows a lot about _____. Stay away from any negatives, like the fact that he would look really good if he dropped 20 lbs. If something is a weakness, leave it off the list. Use these categories as a guide to spur your thinking.

- Physical: looks, stamina, sleep, energy, strength, height, weight, health, and so on.
- Emotional: Justice, mercy, love, tenderness, joy, ability to overcome, kindness, steady, not over-reactionary, and so on.

- Mental: bright, memory, education, curious, wealth of knowledge, wisdom, creative, intuitive, and so on.
- Spiritual: connected to God, awareness, moral, sensitive conscience, and so on.
- Look at the relationships of his life. Which ones are blooming? In what areas is he strong?

God/Spirituality
Personal Development
Marriage
Family
Work
Church/Community of Faith
Money
Society
Friends

## Appreciate important accomplishments.

Another area to mine for respect is by taking a look at the things he has done—his accomplishments. Your husband really wants you to evaluate his present mistakes in the light of all of the good things he has done throughout his life. This tends to be the way men see themselves. They tend to see their lives as a series of events, highlights of good things they have done, usually passing over times of anger, lust, and pride.

Dale Carnegie, in his famous book, *How to Win Friends and Influence People*, shows us that even the worst gangsters think they are pretty good people who were occasionally forced to do a couple of bad things.[1] If this is true of gangsters, then it is even more true for your husband. He desperately needs someone in his corner who will see him from a positive light. He needs his wife to realize that he has accomplished good things and believe he can accomplish more good things.

These accomplishments could be projects, paychecks, vacations, trips, athletic triumphs (even high school feats), notes, purchases, promotions, community involvement, help offered to others, skills developed or demonstrated, team accomplishments, classes taken, degrees earned, jobs held, positions occupied, repairs made, side jobs completed, lectures given, impacting conversations with the children, comfort given in a crisis, or advice that helped a friend or relative.

The fact remains that a man never tires of hearing about or remembering his accomplishments. Even if it has been a long time since he did something nice or productive, he still files it in the permanent "I Did It" file. It can never be taken out. A wise woman helps her husband celebrate the contents of that file, knowing that the celebration gives him energy to accomplish more. A man hopes that his accomplishments swirl around in his wife's mind, creating value and respect that completely dwarf the failures and mistakes of today. This is how respect works with everyone. What a person has done – the positions they hold, and so on – that makes them valuable and respected, hopefully causing you to overlook the small daily foibles and mistakes.

Your husband desperately needs you to build this larger frame of reference to contextualize his recent errors and stupidities. When you look at his life over time, he really has accomplished a number of things that are praiseworthy. Yes, he has some omissions and some errors, but he has accomplished good things with his life. I have had the opportunity to work with a few marriages where the husband committed adultery and broke trust at the deepest levels. The marriages that survived and thrived were the ones where the wife weighed the whole of her husband's life, potential, impact, and accomplishments. She concluded that even though his actions brutalized her soul, he was more than just an adulterer and she was willing to invest in his value again, provided he built reasonable safeguards against this type of sin. Most husbands are doing the best they can and would just like someone to acknowledge in some way all the things they do that contribute to a good marriage, good family, and a better society.

Now, I realize that in the eyes of God measured against His perfect standard, all of us are desperately sinful and selfish and under His righteous condemnation of death. It is also true that God saw value in us and sent His Son, Jesus Christ, to redeem us out of our miserable condition and offer us a significant place in His service. If He was willing to pay for our sins, sees value in us, and places us into His service, then who are we to constantly harp about our husband's shortcomings? It's definitely something to think about.

## Marriage Exercise #3

## Identify His Accomplishments

Identify and write out the various accomplishments of your husband. Use the list below as a prompt to help you think about areas you might not normally consider. You are looking for things that he actually accomplished. It does not matter that he needed help or that he was only a small part of the accomplishment. It can be great fun to have him help you. Have him tell you the top five accomplishments in his life (don't get mad if he doesn't put them in your order). Which one is he most sentimental about? Were there any new ones that surprised you? Avoid comparison. Too often we measure accomplishments against the best in the field or famous people. Whatever he did, it is significant that he accomplished it. Comparing only cheapens it. List out accomplishments in the following areas (if applicable):

45

*Projects*
*Paychecks (size, number, consistency)*
*Vacations*
*Military*
*Education*
*Trips*
*Athletics (teams, triumphs, championships, achievements)*
*Notes, letters, articles, books*
*Positions*
*Purchases*
*Promotions*
*Community involvement*
*Help offered to others*
*Skills developed or demonstrated*
*Team accomplishments*
*Classes taken*
*Degrees earned*
*Jobs held*
*Positions occupied*
*Repairs made*
*Side jobs completed*
*Speeches, presentations, lectures*
*Impacting conversations (children, friends, spouse, colleagues, others)*
*Comfort given in a crisis*
*Other*

**Understand what he refrains from or avoids doing.**
One area that men congratulate themselves for is the stuff that they don't do. This is usually a hidden, internal celebration that wives don't realize they have. Men will compare themselves with others. They may say things to themselves, such as:

*I don't do what Bill is doing when he runs away every weekend from his responsibilities at home by golfing.*

*I don't have a mistress like Jim does.*

*My wife should be grateful for the fact that I give her the paycheck unlike Jerry who blows a good chunk of the money before he ever gets home.*

*I could be working more like Dale does to earn the next promotion, but I don't so that I can spend time with the family.*

These are the types of thoughts that float through a man's mind, so it is helpful every once in a while for a wife to remind herself of all the junk her husband *doesn't* do. Sure, he probably isn't perfect and does a few things that annoy you; but if you focus there, you will overlook a whole lot of things he doesn't do. Not all men will avoid all of the things that are mentioned but realize that there are men out there that do many, if not all, of these things. You most likely have a man who chooses to *not* do many of the sinful options available to him.

I remember one woman who was increasingly angry and displeased by her husband. She saw him as bland and unexciting. "All he wants is to be home," she would say. "He never wants to do anything exciting. Why doesn't he suggest that we go out and have romantic weekends planned?" Eventually she became so disrespectful toward her husband and his boring desires that she divorced him to pursue men with more drive, energy, and excitement. Five years later she was longing for a quiet evening with a man who was thoughtful and interested in family. She had done the bar scene and had been beaten up by exciting men. She had suffered through the "excitement" of venereal diseases. She had "enjoyed" the tension of flirting with men who flirted with everyone in the room. She came to understand the loneliness of

47

being in a room full of people who only care about themselves. She wanted desperately to have her nice, quiet family back; but her disrespect had damaged it so severely that neither her husband nor her children wanted her back. She paid a high price to discover that many men are respectable for what they don't do.

Think about what other men are doing that damages themselves, their wives, their families, and their potential. Get your husband's perspective by asking him what things he refrains or avoids doing because it would not be good for him, for you, or for the family. It should be very eye opening for you and your respect for him will surely grow.

## Marriage Exercise #4

## What Does He Refrain or Avoid Doing?

Write a "yes" by the things your husband avoids. Look at your neighbors, friends, and especially your husband's colleagues. What negative behaviors are they involved in that your husband is avoiding? Admire and compliment your husband for the things he chooses not to be a part of. Ask yourself, "Does he…"

*Avoid getting drunk?*
*Avoid using drugs?*
*Avoid affairs with other women?*
*Avoid yelling?*
*Avoid strip clubs?*
*Avoid and block pornography and sleaze from his computer?*
*Avoid cursing and swearing?*
*Avoid overspending?*
*Avoid behavior that would get him fired?*
*Avoid laziness and sloth?*
*Avoid certain levels of pride, ego, or arrogance?*

*Avoid fighting or belligerent conduct?*
*Avoid unsafe driving?*
*Avoid losing large portions of his paycheck gambling?*
*Avoid loud, unruly friends?*
*Hold back from pursuing activities that would shut you and the kids out?*
*Avoid lying?*
*Avoid violence?*
*Avoid fits of rage and outbursts of anger?*
*Watch fewer sports than he could?*
*Generally pick up after himself?*
*Want a relationship with the children?*

## Appreciate his spiritual gifts.

God has given Christians a number of special abilities that can be beneficial for other Christians and the world at large. It is helpful to take note of these when evaluating the man you are married to. The following verses list and describe the various spiritual gifts: Romans 12:5-10; 1 Corinthians 12-14; Ephesians 4:11-18; 1 Peter 4:10, 11.

If your husband is a Christian, then he has been given special abilities to assist other Christians. God is trying to give him meaning, significance, and purpose in this life. If your husband develops his spiritual gifts, then they will be a rich source of value in his life. There are numerous resources available to assess spiritual gifts, including on-line websites and books. You may want to do an assessment with your husband so you will both know the other person's gifts.

# Marriage Exercise #5

## Spiritual Gift Assessment

Highlight the gifts that you think that your husband might have, even if they are underdeveloped. Realize that these gifts are God-given abilities that prompt him in a particular direction and need to be cultivated. He will begin to progress in new areas and levels of competencies as they are understood and developed.

| | |
|---|---|
| Prophecy | The special ability to convey the truth of God with power, directness, and accuracy. |
| Service | The special ability to be aware of needs and accomplish a task within the community of faith. |
| Teaching | The special ability to explain the truth of God with clarity, insight, and depth. |
| Exhortation | The special ability to come alongside of others and encourage them to solve their problems, to reach their potential, and please God. |
| Giving | The special ability to be aware of needs, the location of resources, and/or to give to meet those needs. |
| Leadership | The special ability to know where God wants a group to go and to draw allegiance from others to help accomplish that goal. In many cases it also includes the special ability to know the steps of action to accomplish the goal and the ability to manage the process. |
| Mercy | The special ability to give comfort, care, and sympathy to those who are hurting physically, emotionally, spiritually, and/or mentally. |
| Wisdom | The special ability to know how to apply information and skill to a situation that will result in a win for God and others involved. |
| Knowledge | The special ability to know or collect the right information and/or skills for a given situation, circumstance, or problem. |

| Faith | The special ability to see what God wants to accomplish and to trust Him for those outcomes that are not yet present or in some cases, not even on the horizon. |
|---|---|
| Healing | The special ability to be aware of physical, emotional, mental, and spiritual problems that God wants to change and the ability to ask God to make the changes. |
| Miracles | The special ability to be aware of those impossible changes that God is willing to make and to ask Him for those changes. |
| Discerning of Spirits | The special ability to be aware of angelic presences, both good and evil, and understand their purpose and steps for removal if they are evil. |
| Tongues | The special ability to praise God in a language either angelic or human that the person does not know. |
| Interpretation | The special ability to translate the praise of God given in a tongue into common language of those around so that others may be edified. |
| Apostle/ Missionary | The special ability to exercise authority over a number of churches and Christians and give direction to them so that God is honored and the gospel is expanded. |
| Helps | The special ability to be aware of needs and provide physical areas of assistance to those in the church and in the community at large. |
| Administration | The special ability to manage and structure an organization for peace, health, and growth. |
| Evangelist | The special ability to share the gospel of forgiveness in Jesus Christ and generate a positive response. |
| Pastor | The special ability to assume the long-term spiritual growth and care for a group of people. |
| Celibacy | The special ability to live a chaste life sexually and enjoy it. |
| Voluntary poverty | The special ability to live at or below the normal standard of living in order to release more resources for the kingdom of God. |
| Martyrdom | The special ability of God to endure physical mistreatment—even death—for the furtherance of the Gospel. |
| Hospitality | The special ability to make people feel welcome and loved. |

51

## Appreciate his personality temperament.

One's personality is defined as their very nature or disposition—it includes their temperament. A temperament is a person's manner of thinking, behaving, or reacting to situations or problems as well as one's usual attitude, mood, or behavior. Many personality weaknesses can actually become strengths if they are developed and used in the proper context. There are dozens of personality profile resources available – each filled with assessments to determine strengths and weakness and a person's temperament. A wife would be wise to familiarize herself with a number of these resources to gain a larger perspective on her husband's positive character traits. Doing so can provide her with much more of an insight into who her husband is; how he thinks, processes information, relates with other people, and so on. This discovery can go a long way toward understanding the reasons why he does the things he does, reacts a certain way, and relates to other people the ways he does and so on. By the way, it would be helpful for her to do some self-assessment too. Self-discovery is always positive and can answer some of the very same questions about her self.

All of us are different. It is helpful to understand that some people gain energy from being with people, while others gain energy from being alone. Some people like to think about abstract concepts, and some much prefer to deal with real-world objects and people. In decision-making, some people are more keenly aware of the impact decisions will have on all the people in their life, and they take that into account when they make decisions. Others, however, have an ability to focus on just the facts or logic of a situation and not worry about its impact on people. Some people have the desire to have closure, planning, and limited unknown variables while others have a desire for spontaneity, new experiences, and the joy of not knowing.

## Marriage Exercise #6

### Personality Temperament Assessment

Pick up a temperament book at a local bookstore and identify your husband's major temperament strengths and weakness. Also identify your own temperament strengths and weaknesses. Often, opposite temperaments attract one another, which can cause tension in the relationship. This is because one person has a hard time understanding the internal impulses of someone who has temperaments opposite of their own. One thing to note is that your husband has temperament strengths, not just weaknesses. It is possible for a wife to identify her husband's temperament strengths as weaknesses because they are opposite to her impulses and orientations. Try to appreciate them for the strengths that they are and the context they shine in. There are many temperament resources available, but some of the more reliable ones include the Keirsey Temperament Sorter and Myers-Briggs. All of them can be found on the Internet or at a local bookstore.

## Lower your expectations to more realistic ones.

One of the greatest causes for anger, depression, and marital trouble is unrealistic expectations. Our expectations tell us whether we think another person has done well or poorly, causing us to be grateful or ungrateful, respectful, or disrespectful. Both men and women can create unrealistic expectations in every conceivable situation, but we have found that many women tend to have unrealistic expectations of their husbands in a variety of areas: how to celebrate her birthday, Valentine's Day, Mother's

Day; the level of participation in household chores; being able to read her mind; and anticipating her needs, wants, desires, and so on. Wives, it is possible for you to create in your mind the way he should act within seconds; and when he doesn't act the way you think he should, you become irritated with him. Ask yourself, "Was it realistic to expect that he act in a perfect manner, given what I told him, how I told him (attitude), his past habits, the situation, or what else he has going on in his life at the time?" With every situation you will tend to create a preview of how that situation should go and how he should respond to you. The temptation will be to picture him as acting perfectly with perfect understanding of all the facts and, therefore, responding perfectly to you. You may be able to anticipate a number of other options:

*He will probably act this way if I say this.*
*He will probably act this way if this person does that.*
*He will never think to do this unless I do or say this.*

The question is this: Which mental picture will you lock on to as your expectation for the interaction?

Now, how do you know if your expectations are unrealistic? The answer lies in whether or not what you wanted or expected to happen actually happened. If not, either the situation would not allow that expectation to be met; perhaps you should have acted differently or shared your expectation more clearly; or your expectation was unrealistic. Friends can be helpful for things like this. Ask them questions like, "Is it reasonable to expect him to do (such and such) at dinner time?" "Wouldn't you expect that a husband who loved his wife would do (such and such) on Valentine's Day?" "Isn't it unreasonable to expect that a wife would put up with a husband who does (such and such)?"

Expecting your husband to read your mind, act like one of your girlfriends, or perform perfectly the elaborate rituals that seem natural to you is probably unrealistic. The quicker you learn how to lower your expectations to what he is really capable of, the faster your respect for him will grow, and the stronger his love will be for you. Instead of laboring over the things he doesn't do perfectly (which can ruin your mood), be thankful for even the smallest of efforts, especially at first. If your husband labors too long under the unrealistic expectations you place on him, he will begin to believe that he is a failure at understanding you and being married. He may withdraw to a safe place like work, friends, or the garage.

You have to realistically ask yourself, "Is my husband (right now) capable of remembering this, or knowing what I like?" Most wives know their husband better than their husbands know themselves. Yet they still create unrealistic expectations of this man as though something happened in his sleep last night that will change him into what they hoped he would be. It is only possible to improve your marriage if you have a realistic picture of the man you are married to. Then you can formulate a way to become a full helpmate to him so that he can reach his full potential.

We are not saying that a woman should not have any expectations or that her husband should not grow and develop to become a better husband, father, citizen, and Christian. But he can't stay under the withering barrage of unrealistic expectations from his wife long term. They destroy him and drain him of energy. Remember that respect is the very energy he needs to motivate him to do his best. So she needs to start with what he is actually capable of doing now, realistically adjusting her expectations of him to the level he is at currently. Then she can start the process of helping him grow to the level she would like to see. It's a process and may take some time, but it is possible.

Leadership is all about getting others to accomplish your externalized expectations. To develop change in him, a wife should use her leadership skills in much the same way a manager would train a new employee. First, she should start by not assuming he knows what she wants. In other words, start at the basics. Then clearly communicate any new expectations in some form or fashion that is easy to for him to understand—through requests, diagrams, suggestions, programs, clear statements, and so on.

Paint a picture for him, describing some of the things you envision for celebrating your birthday, Valentine's Day, or Mother's Day. Show him where he should put his dirty clothes, where you'll set the trash to be taken out, and how you will signal your need for him to empty the dishwasher. Be willing to compliment every step in the right direction and keep being clear and honest with your feedback. Applaud him for his efforts, no matter how small they may seem. If he does it right one time, praise him enthusiastically and show him your genuine appreciation. He will love the approval so much and will strive to get more of it.

## Marriage Exercise #7

## Determine His Abilities

Take the time to actually write out the various abilities that your husband has at this moment. Many times it is easy to overlook the positive skills a man has in the rush to notice what he cannot do. What are the top fifteen things that he does well? What are fifteen things he doesn't do well? Where can your expectations of him change?

### Practice positive, direct requests without criticism or sarcasm.

The key to fostering respect in marriage is to continue kindly communicating our needs and expectations with our spouses without sarcasm or harshness. The joy of living with my wife is that she does not develop unrealistic expectations regarding me. Instead of expecting me to read her mind, she will very kindly ask me if I could assist her with something. When asked this way, it is a delight to help her. At times she will ask me to do something that I should have or could have noticed and done on my own. "Could you take out the trash?" "Would you mind taking this out to the car for me?" Instead of criticizing me for not noticing on my own or taking care of it without her instructions, she values me enough to ask me nicely to help. It is a delight to live with a woman like this.

It is a good idea to eliminate criticism and sarcasm as a way to bring about positive change in a marriage. It does not work. Nothing healthy can come from it. Neither does demanding and ranting. Small changes may take place on the surface to avoid the emotional outbursts, but long-term change does not take place that way. Criticism is usually used to point out desired changes, but continuously pointing out the negative rarely motivates anyone to make the positive changes needed. If your husband needs to change in some way, think through what the positive behavior would look like and not just the negative behavior you want to stop. It is best to be direct, positive, and pointed in requesting a change rather than indirect, negative, and general. He needs you to respect him enough to spell out in clear statements what you need him to do. If you are not ready to describe the positive behavior you want, then you are not ready to request a change.

Too often, we want to point out how irritated or frustrated we are by a particular behavior or omission. But when change is needed, take the time, cool down, and think it through. Be ready to precisely describe the positive behavior that is needed from your husband. For example, "Honey, when you get home, I need you to work with Johnny for fifteen minutes on his math homework. He is struggling right now, and your involvement would motivate him in a new way." Contrast that with this, "I am really tired of your coming home, mauling me, then blobbing in front of the TV, demanding that I bring you snacks." One is motivating and positive. The last – though it may be an accurate statement of what irritates you – does not tell your husband how to solve the problem. It does not help your marriage to think to yourself, "He should just know that I am overwhelmed by all the responsibilities of this house. Why isn't he doing something to help?"

When a wife makes thoughtful requests instead of angry rants, everyone is treated with respect rather than being devalued. When it comes to helping around the house, he probably does not notice how he could pitch in to help. Or he could be afraid of doing the wrong thing or doing it the wrong way, due to past experiences. Another example of this kind of positive, respectful request would be, "Honey, could you take out the trash right now, so I can keep cooking the meal for the evening?" A wife who remembers to put her requests in a specific, positive manner shows respect for her husband, and she will usually get the results she wants.

## Marriage Exercise #8

## Making Positive, Direct Requests

You can practice fine-tuning requests to be more positive and direct. Take each negative response below and determine a new response that is *direct, positive,* and *pointed.* Next time you are tempted to go negative on him, remember this exercise and use your situation to practice. Take note of the results accomplished when you took this new approach.

*"I'm sick and tired of you leaving your dirty dishes all over the house. I'm not your mother!"*

*"Whenever we go out, it would sure be nice if you could get off your cell phone!"*

*"I hate it when you just sit in front of the T.V. all night clicking through the stations. It's like I'm not even here!"*

*"Every time the kids need something, you look at me like I'm the only one who can do it. You're their parent too!"*

*"I hate those stupid video games. Stop playing them and help me."*

### Learn to pay him compliments.

Happy couples appreciate and show gratitude for their spouses, and one way to do that is by paying each other compliments. A compliment is simply an expression of praise, admiration, or congratulation. We all love to be noticed for the good things that we do and the right choices we make. Receiving a compliment for such things energizes and motivates one to do more, all from a simple act of acknowledgment. Every single day a man needs his wife to access his file of all the good and helpful things he's done in his life even though he has likely made mistakes or grievous

59

errors. He needs her to not criticize him, but to positively lead him to his fullest potential. There are some men who will never be great conversationalists or incurable romantics. But can she help him develop his strengths by appreciating him for the other positive areas in his life? Absolutely!

Instead of taking him for granted, dig for reasons to be grateful for the person you married. Too many women measure their husband against some ideal standard like an idealized picture of their father or an image of the perfect husband from a book or TV show. Realize that your husband is a gift to you from God – with all his strengths and weakness. He has areas where he can grow and develop, as well as areas he will not be able to change.

When a wife notices the storms her husband has successfully navigated, she is saying that she loves him and is willing to focus her attention on him. In turn, by pointing out things he has learned or ways he has grown, it gives him more reasons to keep learning and growing. This exercise is designed to lead you in paying compliments to your husband. Since everyone receives a compliment differently, you will have to find the right words or expressions that your husband would appreciate. These questions at least form the basis for these types of things for which to compliment him.

### Marriage Exercise #9

### Paying Compliments

A man needs a woman who will say "thanks" for things like...

*I was just thinking of all the things you could do that you don't!*
Name a few of the things he doesn't do.

*I was just thinking of all the things you have done in your life!*

60

Write 5-10 of these so he knows that you know. He will ask!

*I was just thinking of all the things you have done for me!*
Write 5-10 of these to increase your awareness and gratefulness.

*I was just thinking of all the things you have done for the kids!*
Your willingness to be specific here will allow him to relax, knowing that you notice his efforts and that you focus on what he is doing right, not just what he is not doing.

*I was just thinking of all the ways you have let God use you!*
When you can rehearse the things that you see your husband doing for the Lord, it is a powerful way to show respect and love to your husband.

*I was just thinking of all the ways that you are wired so uniquely!*
It is important that you think about your husband's unique qualities from a positive point of view rather than let a negative view dominate your thinking.

*I was just thinking of all the skills that you have developed!*
If you can go back and realize how many skills your husband has developed and be able to specifically refer to them, it gives weight and power to your show of respect to him. This kind of appreciation of what he has learned to do is what everyone hopes will happen in their lifetime.

*I was just thinking of all the experiences that you have had and the lessons that you have drawn from them. Thanks for going through those and being willing to learn.*
Again, think of specifics.

## Determine how he receives respect.
Different kinds of men need different kinds of respect. There are *strong, dominant, and activated natural leaders* who need lots of

appreciation as the way of giving them respect. It is often difficult to give them this form of respect because it seems that it will only make them busier. What they really need is to be still and enjoy the relationships of the people they love, so some wives have withheld appreciation, trying to get their husbands to appreciate the value of going slow and deepening their relationships. However, this rarely works with this kind of man and usually causes them to work harder and move to other arenas where they can get more affirmation and appreciation. This kind of man will not slow down until they receive a high level of appreciation. They can be led into understanding the value of relationships and rest, but they will not be pushed.

Men who are *life-of-the-party extroverts* need respect in a different way. It is a form of respect that seems most difficult to give them because they already get so much of it. The form of respect they crave is attention. These types of personalities typically announce their presence with everything they do. You demonstrate respect to them when you notice them. Their wives might wish they could tone it down and blend in, but that represents disrespect to this type of person. These men need and want to be the center of attention. A wife of this type of man needs to realize that her husband wants her undivided attention. He would feel respected when she listens to his exaggerated stories and focuses completely on him.

Men who are more *reserved and pleasant* need respect demonstrated to them, not in terms of what they do but in terms of who they are as people and the positions they hold. These are typically not activated people who get a lot done, but they are personalities who want to manage and control the actions of others. They are cautious and sound the note of warnings and concerns. They operate in many ways like brakes on a car—

keeping it from going too fast and allowing it to stop at the appropriate time. This man's wife often wants to respect him, but it is difficult to value him for his cautious approach to life.

Respecting someone because of the position they hold or the quiet, steady, organized manner of lifestyle preferred is difficult at times. These individuals need respect desperately and want their mate to recognize the great value they see in the cautious and efficient studied way they live their life. They need to be respected for the positions they hold and acknowledged for being correct and right because of the title they hold. Many times this type of man marries a woman who is much more motivated to achieve and has high energy. This can cause the wife to evaluate her husband on the basis of her temperament and style of life rather than her husband's very different paradigm.

Lastly, there are men who are *highly analytic and creative*. They want to be appreciated and valued for what they create and think about. They have a desperate need to be understood in the details of their feelings, thoughts, emotions, and desires. To be respectful to this type of man is to be studiously engaged in understanding the person. The greatest thing that can be said to this person is, "I want to understand you." This will be demonstrated by listening and following the conversations and ideas wherever they lead. The wife married to this type of man may think there is never any end to new ideas or his melancholy moods, but to feel respected means his wife pledges to understand him a bit more each day without cynicism or criticism. She must be willing to appreciate him from his frame of reference.

## Marriage Exercise #10

### What's the Best Way?

Think about what description best fits your husband. Different people enjoy praise, respect, and appreciation in different ways. Many men are uncomfortable with open displays of affection so they have a hard time with public displays of gratitude and respect. This does not mean that they do not need the respect or even the displays. I have found that many men will read a note of appreciation over hundreds of time, and they will display a trophy or plaque so they can be refreshed by it on a regular basis. The more specific the praise, appreciation, or acknowledgement of respect, the deeper it will penetrate his heart and the more meaningful it will be.

Spend time today showing your praise, appreciation, or respect in a way that is meaningful to him. Consider writing a note or a verbal compliment, whatever he would receive best. You may have to resort to trial-and-error at first. Just be sure to not take offense if you don't get it right the first time. If you keep at it, you surely will find the very thing that touches his heart. And when you do, you've touched his greatest need for respect.

## Determine how his past experiences shaped him.

His personal experiences have made him the way he is today—wise, thoughtful, disciplined, or productive. Everyone is a mixture of their experiences and how those things have shaped his or her personality. Some of these experiences have been good, while some have been evil. Some have been enriching, others draining. Some of the experiences that he has been through have tilted the floor he is standing on emotionally, mentally, or spiritually. Some men are worthy of praise just for what they have endured in their lives and how "normal" they are in spite of them. Spend some time noting any experiences that had a major impact on his life. You may need to ask him directly to help answer these questions. Write them out in a journal or notebook if you prefer.

### Marriage Exercise #11

### How Have His Experiences Shaped Him?

1. What happened to him from 0-5 years of age?
2. What happened to him from 5-10 years of age?
   * At home
   * In school
3. What happened to him from 10-15 years of age?
   * At home
   * In school
   * With friends
4. What happened to him from 15-20 years of age?
   * At home
   * In school
   * With friends
   * With the opposite sex
   * At church
5. What happened to him from 20-30 years of age?
   * At home
   * In school
   * With friends
   * With the opposite sex
   * At work
   * At church
   * Financially

6. What happened to him from 30-40 years of age?
   - At home
   - In school
   - With friends
   - With the opposite sex
   - At work
   - At church
   - Financially

7. What happened to him from 40-50 years of age?
   - At home
   - In school
   - With friends
   - With the opposite sex
   - At work
   - At church
   - Financially
   - Physically

8. What happened to him from 50-60 years of age?
   - At home
   - In school
   - With friends
   - With the opposite sex
   - At work
   - At church
   - Financially
   - Physically

9. What happened to him from 60-70 years of age?
   - At home
   - In school
   - With friends

- With the opposite sex
- At work
- At church
- Financially
- Physically

## A Note of Caution: Respecting Your Husband Does Not Mean Disrespecting Yourself

Some women allow themselves to be disrespected in the name of respecting their husbands. This cannot be. It does not produce a stronger marriage but actually a weaker one. A strong connection does not take place where there is the impression of a basic inequality in the value of one of the people. Only when husbands and wives respect one another in a godly way can a powerful bonding take place.

A wife is a much more interesting, alluring, and valuable to her partner if she does not allow herself to be devalued. Some men try to devalue their wives through what they say about them, how they treat them, or what they ask them to do. A godly wife cannot allow her personhood to be attacked or degraded. I recommend that wives point out how some of their husband's requests, actions, or speech are not appropriate. She might say something like, "When you do that, say those things, or ask me to do that, I feel disrespected or degraded." While this kind of statement should not be said in anger or with a condemning tone, it can bring a new level of understanding and value, providing needed boundaries to the relationship.

Boundaries are necessary for every good relationship. They should be respected or else the connection will breakdown and the relationship will fall apart. Strong, biblical boundaries are important for every relationship so all the individuals in the relationship are safe and able to express themselves. There may be times in a marriage relationship where a wife may have to firmly hold her ground against her husband if he is trying to force her to violate her conscience or God's law. If you are fearful or in danger in some way, we recommend seeking the help of someone you can trust like a Christian counselor, pastor, or godly friend.

# Chapter 4

# Adapt

*Ephesians 5:22; Colossians 3:18; 1 Peter 3:1; Titus 2:5*

Shelia (not her real name) sat down in my office, angry and frustrated. "I won't divorce him, but I won't be around much either. I just can't stand that he doesn't do anything; he doesn't have any ambition."

After a long discussion with Shelia (and dozens like her), I realized that she imagined a perfect man who is a strong leader at home, has lots of ideas on how to make the family better, is a great conversationalist, and is clearly the spiritual leader initiating godly projects and discussions. She was more than willing to adapt to *that* kind of man. But she was so disappointed by the *real* man she was married to that she was incredibly frustrated and angry.

I asked Shelia to list her husband's strengths and weaknesses. The weaknesses came pouring out, while the strengths took considerable thought. Eventually I asked her to list her strengths and weaknesses. Then I pointed out how so many of her strengths matched his area of weakness and vice versa. I helped her to see that she had aggressive, outgoing gifts of leadership, whereas her husband's leadership gifts were more reserved.

For example, in social situations she had always wanted her husband to be more aggressive and outgoing than she was; but he usually waited for her to introduce everybody, get a conversation flowing, and then jump in from time to time. She wanted him to start his own business using his considerable technical skills and expertise but starting a business was not an interest or competency of his. He knew that he would not enjoy all the responsibilities of owning his own business.

I suggested that she adapt her skills and abilities to help the two of them get along and be successful. She needed to admit to herself whom she had married, stop trying to hope he was perfect, and get on with the business of making her marriage and life work. She protested, saying essentially that she wanted him to be stronger than she was in the area of her strengths. After all, isn't that what the Bible commands the husband to be? I pointed out the contrary—that the Bible tells her to *adapt* to the man God blessed her with. There was no ideal man, other than Jesus, and He remained single.

She had never before considered that her strengths could be the answer to his areas of non-strengths. In other words, she had the ability to use her considerable talents, gifts, and personality to make their marriage strong and powerful. Her eyes were opened, and Shelia received this as new marching orders. Adapting to the husband she had became her new plan.

Her whole mind-set began to change: "If I were to really adapt to him . . . if I were really going to make him successful . . . if I were really going to have a great marriage, what must I do?" She put away the idea that she shouldn't have to do this or that. She stopped thinking he should do this or that on his own. She abandoned the "if she just prayed harder, God would change her husband" strategy. What she found was that as she adapted to the *real* man living with her and began investing herself into his success, their marriage improved dramatically. He felt valued and understood, and *teamwork* was back in the marriage. She and her husband developed a healthy, intimate, and vibrant marriage. They are successful and enjoying life together again.

## The Meaning of Adaptation

In my effort to help Shelia, I realized that she and many wives like her have constructed a perfect man in their minds that they would be willing to adapt to; and they are waiting, practically tapping their feet until he shows up. Some women who find themselves in this place come armed with Bible verses, "Shouldn't my husband do this (or stop doing that) like the Bible says?" and so on. It took me a number of years to realize that this type of complaint was a violation of God's command for wives to adapt; it was actually a form of rebellion.

Now this doesn't mean that the success or failure of the marriage rests solely on the wife's willingness to adapt. Indeed, husbands carry the bulk of responsibility for the marriage in that they are answerable to God Himself for his part in the relationship. God's commandment to husbands is to love his wife as Christ loved the church (God's bride) in a sacrificial, agape-love-kind-of-way (Ephesians 5:25). (Husbands can learn more about this in my book, *God's Radical Plan for Husbands.*) Wives, however, should try to fully engage in the wife role, and she can do that by learning to adapt.

*Adapt* means "to make (something) suitable for a new use or purpose; to modify." Wives can adapt and make modifications to their attitude, position, role, and so forth so as to foster a healthy and prosperous marriage. In the dating phase, adapting to the man you fell in love with may have been natural and easy. It was this

71

ease of which you adapted that likely sold him on the fact that you were the one. It was what allowed you as a couple to move closer together and visualize a future together. A woman in love finds herself making concessions and possibly going to events she would never consider before. She may listen with ease to topics that would typically bore her, agreeing with his argumentation and orientations, and making allowances for his peculiarities.

What neither person counts on is that somewhere between three weeks to two years after the wedding, this natural adaptation and deference stops and now adapting to this man takes a lot of work; indeed, it is some of the hardest work she will ever do. He is no longer the knight in shining armor. His weaknesses and inabilities are glaring. He is even, at times, irritating and seemingly helpless.

When the "auto-adapting feature of dating" turns off, what can wives do at that point? Begin by first understanding that this is a natural event in almost every marriage. Second, determine what kind of a marriage you want to have. Do you want a business relationship where he is emotionally distant and distracted or do you want a close relationship with your flawed but loving husband? You have to choose what you want—the answer determines everything. One way leads to a healthy, vibrant marriage of great joy while the other leads to strife, conflict, and possibly divorce. If a healthy marriage is what you're after, then you can make a conscious decision to adapt to him—to the real man you married.

## Relational Harmony and Peace

A woman who learns to adapt to the uniqueness of her husband will build a magnet that draws him irresistibly. The idea is clear that in order to have a great marriage, you cannot deny the fact of who he is and make him into something he can never be. Instead, you must adapt to him for a common goal.

What does adapting to this man look like so that both of your lives are better? It might be helpful to think of marriage as a way to create beautiful music between two individuals. Adapting to your husband is your contribution to a harmonious team. Harmony means to live in agreement together (in one accord). In terms of music, it is a combination of chords and notes that have a pleasing effect. Where there is harmony, there is beautiful music and dynamic peace. As a wife, you contribute to this amazing symphony whenever you support his efforts and work to bring out his best qualities, adapting to him as needed. However, if you insist on not blending the notes you play to the notes he is playing, the symphony will be a cacophony and painful for all who hear it. If your aim is to get your own way, then the music will be lousy.

Peace does not mean just the absence of war; it means to vibrate in harmony together. A lack of war is obtained in a cemetery, but dynamic peace means that there must be harmony between the things a wife is doing and the things her husband is doing. It doesn't mean that both of you are playing the same notes. Rather, real peace and harmony come when two powerful and dynamic instruments play their notes in such a way to create a beautiful melody, different from either of the individual parts. When one of the instruments refuses to blend or adapt to the other instrument, there is a cacophony of noise and everyone is displeased. For dynamic peace and harmony to occur in marriage, a couple must work together. When this occurs, the relationship has the capacity to be beautiful and enjoyable to the two of you, your family, and others.

During the last few years of my pastoral counseling I found myself asking this question to those who had marital problems:

"What would it take to live with this person in harmony? Let's just say that you adapted to the other person in every way to make them happy and encouraged—what would that look like?" This always sparked a great deal of resistance to the idea at first, but then I would drill in and ask for a specific description of what life would look like if the other person were to be declared the winner. I was interested in whether each person had a clear picture of what the other person was really concerned about or advocating for. Most couples could tell me what life would be like if the other person were allowed to "win" almost all of the time. Then I would ask, "What is so bad about that?" I was interested in how both of them could get the "win."

Often men and women will caricature what the other person needs in a way that is demeaning, degrading, or destructive. "No one in their right mind would suggest that I do that." But instead of reacting to the reality of what they are asking, it is the caricature we react to. The true message gets lost and walls go up. Some couples have stopped listening to each other and instinctively resist anything that comes from the other person.

When couples adopt a competitive view of marriage in which one spouse wins while the other loses, it sets the marriage up for failure. Both parties in a marriage must determine what the other person needs in order to be filled. Marriage is about a couple adapting and learning to allow one's strengths to make up for the other's weaknesses in order to find a way to work together to be healthy and productive. In order to have a vibrant relationship between two people, each must adapt to the other. When that occurs, relational harmony and peace will be achieved.

## Assessing Strengths and Weaknesses

A man, who believes that his marriage, home, and family are

really about his wife more than about him, will naturally tend to withdraw emotionally, mentally, physically, and spiritually from his wife even as she feels things are shaping up in their marriage. If he finds a woman at the office or on the Internet who will adapt to him, he may find himself drawn into an affair for the sheer joy and delight of a woman who will do this. It is not necessarily a younger or prettier woman that steals a husband's heart but rather someone who will admire and adapt to him.

Wives, he needs you to take into account all of who he is and to embrace what that means—both good and bad. Most people have a fear that if someone really finds out what they are like, they will be rejected. A wife who refuses to adapt to her husband unknowingly stamps "rejected" on his forehead, in his mind. When that happens, his greatest fear has been realized—the woman he trusted with the inner part of his life has rejected him. What he hopes is that you will be his friend, which means you will accentuate his positive qualities, abilities, and actions, and help him minimize his incompetence, inadequacies, and mistakes.

The average man realizes he is not complete; he has strengths and weaknesses. He needs someone who will flow into his voids and around his strengths so that together they can be so much more than he as an individual could ever be. He is the man he is. It is the wise wife who takes an honest look at the team she was drafted into and sets about making it a winner, instead of hoping she gets traded to a new team. She also takes an honest look at herself and fills in where he is lacking, allowing him to be strong where he is gifted. The focus is on the health of the marriage, not on personal happiness.

My wife and I are rewarded with a greater intimacy when her strengths are allowed to make up for my weaknesses and vice versa. The longer we are married, the more of these types of adaptations we discover. Sure, she could wish she was married to a perfect person who had no weaknesses or shortcomings; but she has recognized that she is married to me – a real person who has some strengths, some weaknesses, some fears, and some odd behaviors.

## Marriage Exercise #1

## Determining His Strengths and Weaknesses

To realistically assess the strengths and weaknesses of your husband, begin by answering the following questions, perhaps in a journal or a notebook:

*What are five major strengths he possesses?*

*What is he really incapable of? What will he never be like?*

*What activity will your husband never be good at or want to do?*

*What does he need help with? What level of help and assistance is required to bring your marriage, your family, and his career to the next level?*

*What are three areas where you hate adapting to your husband?*

*If you were to adapt to this man and live in his world, taking into account his weaknesses and inabilities, what five things would you do that you are not doing now?*

## Biblical Submission

*Submission* is a word that raises red flags for most women. In fact, it is so threatening for some that they shut out any possibility of understanding the relational insights the word connotes. Biblically, submission is meant for good. Knowing that at some point the willingness to submit would run counter to a woman's

76

natural inclination, God gave wives the command to submit to their husband's authority. It is a hard truth but necessary for a marriage to work the way God intended.

One major aspect of the definition of the word *submission* is "to adapt." The Phillips New Testament translation of Colossians 3:18 reads: "Wives, adapt yourselves to your husbands; that is your Christian duty." By providing this command to adapt (submit), God gives us advanced insight into the relational needs of husbands. It's no wonder that submission and respect go hand-in-hand. A wife refusing to submit is not respecting her husband. It's an important concept to grasp. Read the following verses for greater insight:

- Ephesians 5:22
- Colossians 3:18
- 1 Peter 3:1
- Titus 2:5

This is a tender area for many women because these verses and the concept of submission have been misapplied for centuries. What God intended for good, men have twisted to wound, abuse, and dominate women for centuries. It was never meant in that way but, sadly, that's how it has been used. I believe God gave this command to women because it is a basic relational principle, not because it's His desire for women to play a subservient role.

Again, understand that husbands also have a role in this idea of biblical adaptation. Because they are commanded to love their wives as Christ loves the church, this means that they are to lead her in a compassionate, loving, and sacrificial way. This same love is described in Philippians 2:1-15 and 1 Corinthians 1: Christ's love is sacrificial, compassionate, understanding, considerate, helpful in times of hurt or struggle; it never leaves; it always protects; and always perseveres. The key is wifely

77

adaptation balanced with loving, sacrificial headship by the husband.

Now let me explain why God's commands are hard sometimes. God never asks us to do that which we would do already. He doesn't command us to breathe or to eat or to look out for ourselves. These are things we do automatically. He gives us commands to do what is needed and what we would not normally do on our own. That is why He asks us to love our enemies. That is why He tells fathers not to exasperate their children. That is why He tells us to love one another. God directs us to do what is needed, realizing they would be left undone if it were up to us.

When God looked at the union of two people in marriage, He saw that success in marriage required an adaptation to the husband's leadership on the part of his wife and family. He also saw that, at some point in the marriage, this would run counter to a woman's natural inclinations to want her husband to adapt to her. I believe God saw that if left to her own devices, a woman would naturally strengthen herself and would refuse to adapt to her husband, resulting in a destroyed marriage (Proverbs 14:1). God is good and wants good for you. You can trust Him in this area of adapting.

## Dealing With Expectations

The goal of a marriage is to become a team that accomplishes good things for God, for the two of you, for the children, and for the society. Marriage is not designed so each individual can be deliriously happy. This is the tension in sports—does the athlete focus on getting great individual statistics or having the team win? It is much better to have the team win than to have individual statistics or awards. Either the husband or the wife can refuse to adapt to his or her mate with selfish demands. But if this approach is taken, one person may be happy for a period of time in the midst of a sea of turmoil, and eventually, the marriage will fall apart.

Some couples enter marriage with an inaccurate picture of the person they are marrying or even what marriage is all about. Adapting to a real person for life is different from adapting to a date for an hour or two. Many wives must take a look at their expectations and adapt them to the truth of the person they really married. Real life with the man you married will be completely different from the life you had growing up with your father and your own birth family. You probably didn't think much about the way things worked—that was just the way it was. Now that you are married, you must adapt to a different set of values, ideas, standards, and actions. Some of them may seem unreasonable, but in most cases, they are just different. If you are expecting your spouse to be like your dad, your favorite grandpa, or your pastor, you will be disappointed.

I have talked with hundreds of people in successful marriages, and in every case the wife has a realistic assessment of her husband—both who he is and who he is not. She gives more weight to the things he does well, and she has come to accept what he will never do. She mentally focuses on his strengths and positive contributions, but she is clear about his foibles and weaknesses. She has positively adapted to life with him, and she has decided to give her all to making the marriage, and the man, successful. Let me hasten to add that this does not mean helping him accomplish wickedness or immorality. I write more about that at the end of the chapter. A godly wife adapts to her husband, but she does not adapt to any ways of wickedness to gain a good marriage.

## Avoid Comparison

How does a wife take an honest look at her husband without becoming depressed, or overwhelmed? Avoid comparing. Titus 2:5 makes a specific point that a wife needs to adapt to her own husband, not one that is imaginary or another husband that is not hers. It is the wise woman who focuses on the strengths of her man and praises them, rather than comparing him to some other man. It is imperative that a wife realizes the team she is playing for; and unless her husband is grossly immoral, God wants her to help make the marriage successful. All men are different and come with a wide range of abilities, talents, skills, and physical attributes. The key is to ascertain who they really are and love them for it. Take a minute to think about how your husband relates to the following statements:

*Some men do not have an adequate assessment of their own strengths and weaknesses, while some men are confident and know exactly who they are.*

*Some men are good at doing household fix-it projects, while some men are lousy at this.*

*Some are talkative and good conversationalist, while other men struggle in this area.*

*Some men communicate clearly, while some have a hard time expressing his ideas and feelings.*

*Some men are natural-born leaders, always in charge; others never take the lead.*

*Some men like exploring new ideas, while others prefer to refine existing things.*

*Some men naturally make lots of money; some work hard but barely make ends meet.*

*Some men need lots of attention, while others are uncomfortable talking about themselves.*

*Some men are physically fit and athletic, while others have little coordination or muscle.*

*Some men are brilliant and philosophical, while others only like discussions about real situations and people.*

*Some men are critical and demanding, while others are generous and magnanimous.*

*Some men have chiseled good looks, while others have to smile to look passable.*

I am concerned that the concept of teamwork in marriage has been replaced by, "If I just marry the right person, I can kick back and enjoy the wonders of a great marriage." This is not how a great marriage happens. Every man has his flat spots. God has called the majority of men and women to be in a partnership called *marriage* to complete them and to bring about a level of success that is simply not possible without the other person. Your husband is counting on you to understand him, to grasp the context in which he lives, and to bring what is needed to the marriage so the glow of success will be all over your life. Too often women hold back or wait until their husbands make some kind of improvement, or they retreat into a "fantasy land" of romantic novels and "knights in shining armor." The marriage you are in needs your work; it needs the gifts and skills you uniquely bring to it. All you have is needed to bring about a winning team.

A number of years ago I counseled a couple that was in deep trouble in their marriage. We will call them Bill and Sally. When I was called in, they were talking about divorce and rehearsing the problems they had. According to them, they were just incompatible. Maybe they should not have gotten married in the first place. Each person began the process by trying to get me to agree with a certain point of view against his or her spouse who was being unreasonable. When I looked beneath the surface, it really was a series of small things that kept being escalated into discussions of separation and divorce. She saw him as lazy and underachieving. He saw her as an unrelenting nag who never let him enjoy being home. He was a hardworking man, bringing home an adequate paycheck.

One of their complaints centered around the household activity on Saturday mornings. When she was growing up, her father was always up early, working around the house. Everybody in the family had to pitch in and do chores. When he was home, her father moved from one fix-up project to another. This was the way she imagined the ideal family . . . just like her family growing up.

Bill, however, enjoyed a totally different kind of Saturday during his early years. His family always slept in and lazed around most of the morning, eating pancakes and watching cartoons. Saturdays were his time to sleep in and just "hang out." In his mind, nothing of significance would happen until after 12:00 on Saturday. He had earned this right to take the morning off and, besides, it just felt right. He did notice, however, that his wife would get increasingly upset if he was leisurely enjoying himself, and that she was increasingly pleasant and energetic if the home was a beehive of activities and chores.

When we were able to talk about the ideal Saturday morning and where each one's ideas came from, it was not all that difficult to bring a new level of harmony to the marriage. Sally saw that Bill worked hard all week, and that he deserved a chance to sleep in and laze around if that was what he wanted. Bill saw her need to get chores and household things done on Saturday and relax later. Sally also saw that she was evaluating Bill against the activities of her father. She had adapted to her father rather than her husband. Eventually she came to realize that her father, while "almost perfect" in the chore department, did not have long conversations with anyone in the family or rarely took time to just have fun. Her husband, Bill, was very good in the conversation department and was a lot of fun even though he was not as good in the chore department. With her perspective changed, she was able to adapt to the husband she married and found that she had a very good man.

One of the things I tell people constantly is, "There are always options." Options usually include what both parties are looking for. When two people reach an impasse in their marriage, it suggests that both people have a perspective that needs to be included in the final solution. Only rarely have I seen situations where an individual's ideas must completely be declared wrong. On those rare occasions – usually if it was handled right – even they could see that their original ideas needed to be abandoned in the light of new information. If a wife is willing to be creative or surround herself with helpful, creative people, there are almost always ways to adapt to the ideas, directions, and actions of her husband in a God-honoring, positive way.

Let me introduce you to Jim and Barbara. This couple did not have a good marriage. They fought all the time and had completely different points of view about many things. He was clearly an irreligious person who enjoyed drinking and being in charge. Barbara also liked being in charge. She was a devout Christian who did not appreciate her husband's lack of interest in God, the church, and the way he mocked her beliefs to the children. I was shocked when she told me that Jim had asked if they could come and see me for marriage counseling.

The couple was at an impasse. She wanted to stay home to raise the children and tend to the house. His job had too many times of ups and downs to make the finances steady. He wanted her to get a job, but she adamantly refused. She was willing to push this to the wall. Caring for the children was more important than money. This was just the latest argument in a relationship filled with contrasting opinions. I made them say exactly what they thought was best for the family and why. Then I asked if they could see any way to put the two of them together.

Neither one of them could come up with a way to combine the different visions for the family. It was either he wins or she wins. I asked them to spend a week thinking about any ways they could put the two of these things together. They still couldn't come up with any ways. It had settled into a "no-compromise," "who is the winner" case, and I, as the pastor was supposed to decide. I asked Jim, "It doesn't matter what she does as long as she is working, right?" "Yes," he responded. I then asked Barbara, "Is the main thing for you to be with the kids?" "Yes," she replied.

I let them know I had done research on this issue and found a Christian school near their house that was looking for a new teacher in their oldest child's grade. They didn't pay much, but it was steady and the children of a teacher went to the school tuition-free. I had already put in a recommendation for Barbara at the school. She could call for an interview if she was open to it. This resulted in a win for everyone. She adapted to the different way of solving the problem without making her husband the loser. Also, she gained valuable input into her children's lives and enriched her marriage significantly.

# How Can You Adapt to Your Husband?

Does adapting have anything to do with being a leader? No. In fact, some of the best leaders in history have adapted to the people and situations around them. Great leaders have been known to exercise their leadership under others' authority. For example, the overall leader of the Allied forces in World War II was Omar Bradley, but the two generals who did the greatest job of leading were Dwight Eisenhower in the North Atlantic and Douglas Macarthur in the Pacific Theater. These men did not need to be the supreme leader to lead. They were given an assignment and, to the best of their abilities, led from the second position. Biblically, Joseph was one of the best leaders in the Scriptures. Yet in each part of his life, his leadership was under the direction of a person above him.

In many marriage-counseling situations, I have asked wives to lead their marriages to success in the areas where their husbands are weak. Those wives who have taken up the challenge to exercise their full leadership potential for their marriage have been rewarded with a great marriage. Some women wait in vain for their husbands to pour all their energy into the marriage and family or for them to develop a form of leadership they will just never develop. Some women refuse to assist, lead, or strategize on how to maximize their husband's strengths for the good of the family. These women have an "all-or-nothing" view of leadership. Either he is the out-front, vocal, aggressive leader or he isn't the leader at all. This is a faulty view of how leadership works and how teams win. Real leadership, in almost any endeavor, is a group process where the person who is commissioned with the leadership role is surrounded by a group of people who maximize the leader's strengths and minimize the weaknesses.

I can remember a two-week period where I was counseling

three different couples in which each of the wives had strong leadership gifts. Each of these couples were struggling and fighting, and the wives were contemplating divorce. When I challenged each of these women individually to adapt to the men they were married to and lead under his broad guidance, their marriages took a dramatic turn for the better. I remember one of these ladies had complained for years about her husband's lack of spiritual growth. Within two week after challenging her to use her leadership skills to indirectly assist his spiritual growth, I received a formal request from the company where her husband worked to conduct a Bible study once a week at lunch. He came home and told his wife that the pastor was going to be teaching a class at work on Mondays. He began to grow spiritually, and it changed the nature of their marriage. She had led behind the scenes to bring about a new level of spiritual growth in her husband and her marriage.

In order for a marriage to work, I have found that all of the best qualities from both partners are required. To biblically adapt means to figure out how to make the other person successful and what your part in that process entails.

## Adapting to His Ideas

Many women have asked me, "Why won't he come home and spend time with us?" It is possible that their lack of family interest could be tied to the fact that at work he has value and respect, and people pay attention to his ideas and plans. People at work adapt to him. At home, his wife and children may expect him to fit into a well-defined role they have created for him. I have watched many men exit or balk at being engaged in their family if there is not a willingness on the part of their wives to adapt to them and their leadership. Many wives don't understand this, but a man will opt out of his marriage and family if it is clear that his ideas, his plans, and his presence—with all his strengths and weaknesses—do not make him a major player at home. He will see it as a renegade factory where he is not wanted.

Many men opt out of family involvement because they feel their ideas are resisted, changed, or ridiculed. Their distance may come in the form of working more hours, improving their golf game, or finding some other pursuit because they do not feel welcome in their own homes. I know many wives will complain that their husbands have not asserted themselves. In looking at this need from a number of different angles, I have begun to ask, "Would a man want to spend more time with a family who doesn't understand him nor like his ideas? Or would he want to spend time at work where people are waiting for his ideas, and with friends who allow him to have weaknesses and odd behaviors?"

If none of a husband's ideas are incorporated into the household—how it looks, how it runs, etc. – then it may cause him to "feel" invisible. Most men will not stay where they are invisible—it's just not in their nature. I am amazed at the extreme sensitivity some men have when their ideas, directions, and expectations are resisted. It does not take much for a man to feel he is being resisted. Many wives do not even realize that their questions, tone, and demeanor have been interpreted as resistance. Ask your husband to give you two or three examples of when he feels you have resisted his ideas, and you will see his sensitivity to being resisted.

To create a safe environment for your husband's involvement, be positive and encouraging about his ideas and directions. Listen when your husband suggests preferences or ideas. It is not essential that everything he says be adopted, but it is essential that you try to understand his perspective and orientation. Some things he talks about will be passing fancies; others will come from the core of his being. He may just be trying to have a discussion about it. It takes attentive listening to determine which is which. Adjustments and changes to be made can be discussed later.

## Marriage Exercise #3

### Incorporating His Ideas

If you feel your husband is not engaging in the home and family, try answering the following questions as truthfully as possible. They may be difficult to digest and are not meant to be a list of marching orders. Rather, we ask provocative questions that will get at the root of the problem so it can be addressed.

- *If your husband were to describe the ideal house, how would it be? What would your house look like if your husband had complete say on how it was decorated?*
- *Do any of his ideas or thoughts show up in your home?*
- *What would be different if your husband had complete control over spending?*
- *Are any of his ideas on spending implemented?*
- *What would be different about the children if his plans for their clothing, behavior, schooling, and discipline were implemented fully?*
- *Which actions of your children most annoy or trouble your husband?*
- *How different would your schedule be if your husband were completely in charge of it?*
- *What aspects of your schedule reflect his ideas?*
- *If your husband could pick your friends, would anything change? Would anything change in your friendships with others if your husband had his way?*

- *If your husband were to describe the ideal weekend, what would it look like?*

- *What are some options your husband would like to add to your weekly schedule?*

## Adapting to His Work

One of the tension points between husbands and wives is his work and its demands on him. His career is not an add-on appendage to his life that spits out money every other week. Rather, it is a huge part of who he is and what he is all about. Men invest a considerable amount of time, energy, resources, and ego at work, spending eight to fifteen hours per day, five to seven days a week.

With this in mind, if a wife is going to build a great marriage, she must understand his work in all its complexities. If she does not, she will not be close to him. This can be challenging particularly if the work he does is not interesting to her. Even so, her adaptation to his career is crucial to the health of their marriage. That may involve just listening to him debrief when he comes home. Or it could involve his travel, a bizarre schedule, listening to sad tales of the people, dinner parties, or actual participation in the business. It will look different for everyone.

I remember hearing about a woman whose husband was a radiologist at a local hospital. She seriously thought he worked on radios every day. I have heard countless men complain that their wives have no idea how hard they work or the stress they are under. Most men are hoping, wanting, and even praying for a decompression time and a relief of stress from work when they are home. One way they do this is by talking it out with their wives.

I have watched as wives glaze over with boredom when he begins to discuss the people, pressures, and particulars of his work. If this is your tendency, try this experiment: Go for a walk with

89

your husband; be willing to let him talk about his work the entire time. I guarantee it will make a difference in your relationship. After all, this is his world for the better part of every day. A great marriage does not emerge when that part of his life is put on an island and completely divorced from his home life.

I had the privilege of working with a number of marriages where the husbands worked for the government in secret projects, and they were not allowed to talk about anything at work. This made it difficult for the men to be real because they had nothing they could talk about that really affected or interested them. This almost always was detrimental to their marriages.

Some women are unwilling to admit that their husbands have the work schedule they do. They want them to have a typical 9 to 5 job. Every career has some quirks, whether it is farming, banking, sales, medicine, ministry, law, business, politics, teaching, coaching, and so on. There is no ideal job that doesn't make demands on your time while giving you a living wage in return. The only one I know is called retirement, and it can be boring or limited in its living wage.

Most men are not like the ones on television. It would be nice if he came home at the same time every day, had lots of energy for the family, had troubles at work only once per season, and never needed his wife's help or support. But usually the reverse is true. I remember one man in sales telling me that it would be easier to handle the rejection he faces at work every day if his wife sent him off to start his day with love, tenderness, and encouragement, instead of demands, anger, and a recitation of his mistakes.

A great marriage involves his expressing his emotions, ideas, and passions and a wife's undying support. So much of that involves supporting his work, even if his work is not something he likes. He needs a woman who will do all she can to adapt to his

90

work life and all it entails. Men are often tempted by a woman at the office because she is involved deeply in the world he lives in and has adapted herself to have value in that world.

## Marriage Exercise #4

### Adapting to Promote Success at Work

If your husband were to do a good job at his firm (enough to get promoted or a raise), what would his work schedule look like? Fill out the weekly time schedule or ask him to fill it out. What would it take for him to get ahead at work? How could you make it easier for him to accomplish that level of involvement?

|          | Mon. | Tues. | Wed. | Thurs. | Fri. | Sat. | Sun. |
|----------|------|-------|------|--------|------|------|------|
| 6 a.m.   |      |       |      |        |      |      |      |
| 12 p.m.  |      |       |      |        |      |      |      |
| 12 a.m.  |      |       |      |        |      |      |      |

## Marriage Exercise #5

### Adapting by Involving Yourself in His Work

Some women put up with, but never truly embrace, their husband's chosen career. It is fashionable today for a wife to see herself as having an independent life apart from her husband's career. In our modern world, many women think they do not need to adapt themselves to their husband's career; but in actuality, he may need you to adapt by participating in client dinners, socials, parties, photo ops, appearances, speeches, lifestyles, and so on. If

91

you were to adapt to your husband's career, what could you do to enhance your participation through appearances, involvement, interaction, etc. What would it look like? I know a number of wives and husbands who did not sign up for what their spouse is doing now and it's demanding on them. But those with great marriages adapt by throwing themselves into the new duties and involvement for the sake of the marriage.

## Adapting to His Leadership

There are two myths regarding leadership in marriage. One is that women have no leadership abilities, and the second is that submission means you never exercise your leadership gifts or abilities. Myth number one is patently false. God has invested men and women with varying levels of leadership abilities. He wants every person to exercise the gifts, talents, and abilities He has given for the advancement of His will. Let's take a brief look at a couple of women in the Bible who exercised leadership:

- Deborah, the judge, exercised great leadership gifts (Judges 4).
- Mary, Jesus' mother, exercised her leadership at the wedding in Cana when she directed the headwaiter and his servants to do whatever Jesus told them to do (John 2:1-11).
- Lydia, a merchant of purple cloth, provided hospitality for Paul, Silas, and Timothy (Acts 16:13-15).
- Phoebe was a deaconess for the early church (Romans 16:1).
- Others include: Sarah, Priscilla, and Mary Magdalene

Since God has clearly given women leadership gifts, it is obvious that He wants women to use them. Our culture tends to think of leadership as taking charge, being noticed, having positions of power, and having a commanding presence. This, however, is not the essence of *godly leadership*. Godly leadership does not demand power, attention, or position to exercise its energy. Rather it is a leadership that is humble, servant-oriented, and selfless.

One of the complaints from many wives is that their husbands will not be the leaders of the home the way they are supposed to be. For years I believed men were to be the hands-on directors of all the activities of the home life. I invested a lot of time, energy, and resources to try and motivate men to assume this role in their families. It did not work. I have since come to understand a different view of a man's leadership in the home.

It might help to think of him like the owner of a series of companies in which he places the best leaders he knows to run individual companies. He gets reports regularly about the companies and how they are doing. He meets with each of the leaders of the separate companies to monitor their progress and give general direction. The owner lays out the broad goals and strategy for the year, allowing the details to be mapped out by the individual leaders of the various companies. He will inject himself in the company at various points in order to help out or fulfill significant responsibilities, but his lack of day-to-day management and detailed leadership does not mean he is not the leader.

What I have come to understand is that God has equipped women with leadership gifts they should use to accomplish the family's goals. Most men are more than willing to be involved in the family's organization as it is moving to accomplish the agreed-upon goals. A wife can and should adapt the exercise of her gifts of leadership to complement her husband's gifts, style, and level of leadership. She will do herself, her family, her husband, and Christ a great service if she uses all the leadership abilities she has been given.

The key to a great marriage is to realize that leadership in marriage is not the same as business, where ability displaces some and promotes others. A marriage is about relationship and accomplishment. If something is accomplished but the achievement destroys the relationship, it is not successful. Let me give you a couple of examples. If a wife gets the right drapes but her husband felt he was manipulated to get them, then the leadership was a failure. Or, if she volunteered him for something that he resents giving his time for, then her leadership has damaged the relationship.

On the other hand, if there are good relationships but nothing is achieved, the family is also a failure. His leadership position and her leadership abilities must be combined together to make sure both issues are accomplished: relationship and accomplishment. Our capitalistic culture has the idea that unless one enjoys the top position, one cannot exercise leadership. History and Scripture differ with this assessment. Good leadership is essential at every level of a successful organization. I have found some of the greatest advancements in a marriage happen when both parties begin exercising their unique leadership skills in concert with one another.

I remember hearing about a group of women who got together to discuss how weak and spineless their husbands were. These sessions did not improve anybody's marriage, and they began to find new flaws in their husbands. They would plan ways to antagonize and irritate them. These kinds of gripe sessions never produce a better marriage. It may allow you to get a few things off your chest but cementing negative thoughts about your husband will not help you build a great marriage. It turns you into a cynic and impacts the acceptance and encouragement he needs from you.

# Marriage Exercise #6

## Adapting to His Leadership

Some men are maintainers and not initiators. Initiators are viewed as leaders in our culture, but this is not the only kind of leadership there is. Some are very good at implementing other people's ideas, some are good at managing, and some are good at refining an existing process. A man brings all he is into his marriage. What kind of leadership does your husband naturally express?

1. If your husband were the leader of the following areas, what would it look like?
   - Home—
   - Finances—
   - Children—
   - Friends—
   - Recreation—
   - Church—
   - Community involvement—

2. In what settings have you seen him take the lead?

3. How does he usually prefer to express his leadership? Directly or indirectly (through you and others)?

4. What kind of leader is your husband?
   - Initiator vs. Controller
   - Aggressive vs. Cautious
   - Personal (hands-on) vs. Delegating (through others)
   - Dominant vs. Laissez-faire
   - Upfront vs. Behind-the-scenes

5. How does the average woman resist her husband's leadership? Look at the list below and see if you have been guilty of any of these subtle forms of rejecting his leadership. If you have, plan

to draw him out and be more of a team with him.

- Taking his discussions and/or ideas too personally
- Jumping to conclusions about what he means or drawing conclusions about what it would mean to you
- Shutting down his ideas too quickly
- Not looking for the root intention
- Ignoring his ideas
- Rejecting his ideas
- Changing his ideas too quickly
- Only being interested in discussing your ideas
- Only wanting to implement your ideas
- Believing that it is your vision for the family that must be implemented
- Believing that it is your vision for the house that must be acted upon

### Marriage Exercise #7

### Adapting to His Personality

Everyone has a group of traits or tendencies that "feel" right to them. Taken together, these are called our personality – both the good and the bad aspects. Ask yourself the following questions and take an honest look at the man you married:

*What are the strengths of his personality?*

*What are the weaknesses of his personality?*

It can be helpful to read a few temperament or personality books to get a list of various temperament traits.

# Marriage Exercise #8

## Adapting to His Phobias

Gary Smalley, in his wonderful book, *The DNA of Relationships*, lists 25 fears that destroy marriages. Look at this list and circle the ones that seem to be animating your husband at times. If your marriage is at a place where you can ask your husband to discuss this list with you, ask him to suggest which ones are his dominant fears.[1]

| | |
|---|---|
| Rejection | Inferiority |
| Judgment | Worthlessness |
| Disconnection | Feeling Disliked |
| Loneliness | Mistrust |
| Failure | Despair |
| Powerlessness | Feeling Devalued |
| Condemnation | Humiliation |
| Feeling Unwanted | Abandonment |
| Danger | Feeling Unimportant |
| Being Misunderstood | Feeling Ignored |
| Being Scorned | Neglect |
| Being Invalidated | Unhappiness |
| Feeling Defective | |

## Marriage Exercise #9

## Adapting to His Background & Experiences

Every man has had a series of good and bad experiences that have helped shape him into the person he is today. These are the reasons why he acts the way he does. Write out major positive or traumatic events in each period of his life. Then, go back and look at the impact and power of those events. In what ways could you adapt to those events in his life? What is the power in those events that still impacts him today?

| Age Groups | Major Positive or Traumatic Events |
|---|---|
| 0 - 10 | |
| 11 - 20 | |
| 21 – 30 | |
| 31 – 40 | |
| 41 – 50 | |
| 51 – 60 | |

| 61 – 70 | |
|---------|---|
| 71 – 80 | |
| 81 - 90 | |

## Marriage Exercise #10

### Adapting to His Culture

He doesn't think about his culture—it is just what seems right to him. This comes from his ethnic heritage, his family heritage, and his surroundings. Look at the areas listed below and write the things he does or expects that seem right to him, especially those that don't seem right to you. For example: it just seems right for dinner to be at 5 p.m. or it just seems right for women to do the dishes.

*Home:*
*Family:*
*Marriage:*
*Work:*
*Church:*
*Finances:*
*Vacation:*
*Recreation:*
*Men's roles:*
*Women's roles:*

## A Warning About Over-Adapting

It is important to say that a wife should never adapt to something criminal, immoral, or unethical. She is a child of God before she is the wife of any man. If the core of what her husband is asking her to do is illegal, unethical, or immoral, she must obey the higher law (Acts 5:29). Adaptation does not mean a loss of personhood, self-respect, or participation in criminal behavior. Adaptation is essential to building a great team so a marriage and the family can be maximally effective. But over-adapting is destructive to the relationship and the individual. A woman needs to be honored and respected in order to have a great marriage. This means that at times she must say "I will not do that or be involved with that because I feel degraded or disrespected by that activity."

A wife should not adapt to being demeaned, abused, or devalued. There are often options that will accomplish a husband's intent without including the criminal, immoral, or unethical. On those rare occasions where he will not accept any options other than involvement in that which is evil, a higher law must be obeyed. Good marriages, and good teams of any kind, must major on adaptation to each other so the goals of the team can be accomplished. There may be things that cannot be adapted to and so a stand must be taken.

## What Does Over-Adapt Mean?

In some cases there is the problem of wives choosing to over-adapt or being asked to over-adapt. Adapting that takes away individuality, personhood, or self-worth is considered to be over-adapting. Adapting that requires lockstep thinking is over-adapting. Adapting that requires sin is over-adapting. A wife is never called upon in Scripture to become a non-person, a slave, or a criminal to fulfill her role as a wife. She needs to adapt within the boundaries of righteousness, a healthy relationship, and her marital goals.

I remember working with a woman who over-adapted by allowing her husband to get her involved in pornography to pay the bills. By the time they came to see me, their marriage, finances, and her conscience were a mess; and he still did not understand why. This is over-adapting.

I also remember working with a woman who adapted too much by allowing herself to be beaten physically when her husband was not pleased with something she did. She did not begin to heal until she reported his behavior to the police and sought the help of a domestic shelter. A wife cannot, and should not, adapt to her husband if it means to participate in sin, perversion, or wickedness or if it involves the surrender of her personhood, domination, or subjection in such a way as to suggest that she is less than he is and not an heir of the grace of life.

If in reading this you feel you may be over-adapting in an unhealthy way, please seek the advice of a pastor, godly counselor, or friend right away.

# Chapter 5

## Domestic Leadership

*Titus 2:4-5; 1 Timothy 5:14*

The beginning of the turn-around in Bill and Sally's marriage took place when Bill got injured at work and had to be home for a few weeks. Unfortunately their marriage had to get worse before it got better. I would love to tell you that when Bill injured himself, he became tender and kind and that their marriage enjoyed a powerful recovery. He eventually did become more tender and kind, but that did not happen until much later; and it was not what triggered their marital recovery.

Instead, their marriage made a significant change for the better when Sally adjusted some things she had been doing. It was a change in her that triggered a growing difference in Bill, allowing them to get on the same page together. She had been telling Bill for years that she did not have enough time in her day to get everything done. Bill repeatedly pleaded and even demanded that she handle certain things about the family and around the house because of his work schedule. He needed her to deal with the kids in a certain way so that the house wasn't in chaos when he got home. He needed her to keep a level of cleanliness and neatness in the home, arrange certain appointments, and fix certain problems during normal business hours while he was at work.

When Bill was injured and laid up, he was in the bedroom and could not get out of bed easily. After a while, she forgot about his being there as he was in and out of consciousness. Sally began to settle back into her normal routine. As his health improved, he was more alert and took notice of how she spent her time. From the back bedroom he began to keep a log of what she did all day. I remember his coming to counseling and reading the log. "She spent four hours on the phone with her friends yesterday," he exclaimed. "And the days before that were just about the same. She says that she doesn't have any time, but she wastes a lot of time on the phone. I need her to actually engage here at home." He pointed out that if he tried to do her schedule at his work, he would be fired. "I need a partner who is working as hard as I am."

Hearing his words stirred a wake-up call in her soul. Once she realized that she would be fired if she were working for a regular company, she knew she had to change her perspective. In the most important company of her life (her marriage and family), she was a terrible employee, a terrible manager, and had set her schedule as though she were a person on vacation instead of the leader of the household. She remembered the agreement they made before they had children—she would stay home to provide the stability and nurture that the children needed. She admitted that after a while, she was lulled into a selfish use of her time instead of a focused attention on the development of their marriage and family. She had forgotten that her role was central to the enjoyment and long-term success of their marriage and family. She was literally in charge of their family while he was away trying to earn enough to fund this vital enterprise.

Though this can be a difficult topic between men and women today, the truth is that a man has a need for his wife to be every bit the leader she can possibly be in the domestic arena. Even if she also works outside the home, her husband will likely look to her to express huge levels of leadership in the area of home and family. The greater a man's need for domestic leadership from his wife, the more he will usually hint or insist that his wife stay home to care for the children. This need in men has been ridiculed and shamed to a place that men often won't talk about it anymore. Though it may seem old-fashioned and in some circles "sexist," it is still a deep-seated need and desire for men to have their wife manage the domestic area. Men long to come home to a well-maintained home with respectful and expectant children. Even though our culture is fighting against this picture, the need in men is still there.

Willard Harley, a successful marriage and family therapist, states:

*"So deep is a husband's need for domestic support from his wife that he often fantasizes about how she will greet him lovingly and pleasantly at the door, about well-behaved children who likewise act glad to see him and welcome him to the comfort of a well-maintained home. The fantasy continues as his wife urges him to sit down and relax before taking part in a tasty dinner, its aroma already wafting through the air.*

*A lot of wives chuckle as they read the above scenario, but I assure you it is quite common in the fantasy lives of many husbands...The male need for his wife to "take care of things"—especially him—is widespread, persistent, and deep. I don't see it changing..."*[1]

## Biblical Insight

Two verses in Scripture deliver this point: 1 Timothy 5:14 and Titus 2:4-5. Both verses address one of the primary functions of wives—to manage the domestic arena. Domestic leadership is a part of God's job description for wives in that He places incredible value on the functionality and health of home-life. He delegates this important role to wives, not because it is easy or fun, but because He uniquely gifted them with certain abilities to manage this area as well as a naturally nurturing spirit to make the home special and alive. Think about it, if it wasn't for a wife's special touches around the home or the extra effort she puts in around the holidays, life would be dreary, plain, dull, and sparse. Security and peace at home meets one of the deepest longings of a man, which in turn provides for a stable marriage and family. It's a primary component of what draws a husband home every day.

In Titus 2:4-5, God says that young women should be instructed "...to love their husbands, to love their children, to be sensible, pure, workers at home, kind, being subject to their own husbands, so that the word of God will not be dishonored" (NASB). The idea of "workers at home," as Titus 2:5 describes, can be explained further when we look at the original Greek. The word *oikourgos* is made up of two words—*house* and *work*. It literally means laboring or working in or about the house. God is clearly saying to wives, "You don't understand how important this is, but you need to throw yourself into making your household work well." There is no notion of the idea of a kept woman in this verse. It describes significant work and a role, which needs clarity and understanding.

In 1 Timothy 5:14, the Apostle Paul again speaks to young widowed women, who are not married, about the responsibilities in marriage, "I want younger widows to get married, bear children, keep house, and give the enemy no occasion for reproach" (NASB). The words "keep house" is the Greek word *oikodespotein,* which is made up of two words combined—*oikos* (house) and *despot* (leader or boss). It literally means that the wife is to be the house despot or leader. This was not confinement to some backwater assignment; rather, it should be viewed as a serious leadership role that is crucial to the success of any marriage and family. In the ancient world, home was the place out of which the whole of life sprang. It was a place of business, learning, security, and success; the center out of which all of life was operated.

Why are the young women to be instructed in this way? We remember from the previous chapter that God commands us to do the hard things we need to do for our benefit and the benefit of others rather than relying on what we want to do. Plus, there is an even deeper reason, one that has Kingdom implications. The Bible tells us in Titus 2:5 and again in 1 Timothy 5:14—so that the word of God will gain added value in the eyes of society. In other words, it bears a favorable witness to Jesus and His followers when we live in such a way that gives the enemy no cause for criticism.

You might be asking yourself how managing your household could have such a far-reaching impact as the Scriptures connote. It might be helpful to understand that at the time they were written, the Christians lived in a largely pagan society where the women worshipped goddesses who advocated female dominance and power over men. Under the inspiration of the Holy Spirit, the Apostle Paul instructed Christian wives to live differently—to be godly and reverent to their husbands and their marriages. Though this may seem old-fashioned or unfair in today's day and age, it is actually in line with godly living—it has a godly purpose, as it represents living differently than what the culture values.

## Choices, Choices

In His wisdom, God uses Paul's instruction to address a danger that all women through the ages have faced. Just like in ancient times, women today are faced with a number of options in which to direct her energies. She can work outside the home; volunteer in the church, community, and the kids' school; go back for more education; pour into an interest or hobby; focus on external friendships and relationships, etc. The choices are endless and many are very rewarding and validating. It's no wonder that her home may be the last place she wants to put in loads of energy and time.

You might be interested to know that women (and men, too) have nine basic relationships that make up life. In order of priority, they are: God, Self, Marriage, Family, Work, Church, Money, Society, Friends. All nine of these relationships are crucial to a fully developed life. But there is a temptation to spend too much time, energy, or resources on one of the other relationships to the detriment of the crucial duties at home. This is especially true in the modern world where the home seems like the most boring of all places to invest one's energy.

The verses we studied direct wives to learn to focus a significant percentage of their energy to leadership at home, rather than all the other distracting things that could capture your skills and abilities. They instruct young wives to learn how to focus their skills on productive activities that will develop a great marriage and a great family instead of putting a lower priority relationship ahead of a higher priority relationship. It is not that a wife cannot have secondary activities and interests, but there must be a focused attention on the most important relationships first.

As a side note, notice that marriage comes before family in order of priority. Many wives make the mistake of putting all of her energy and time into the children and neglecting the relationship she has with her husband. What often happens in many marriages is that when the children leave home, there isn't much of a relationship left between the husband and wife. This is a time when many couples are most vulnerable for divorce. Wives, as the house leader, schedule time and activities in your life that demonstrate the value you place on the marriage relationship. Don't make the mistake that many women make—assuming he will always be there.

## A Call To Wives

By now you probably grasp that a wife's leadership at home is essential to the development of a great marriage and family. Even though at times it may seem thankless, anonymous, or endless drudgery, it is exactly where your attention, time, and energy are needed most. Your leadership and the marshaling of resources under your direction are essential to bring about the success of your marriage and family and should be your number one priority.

God is calling on wives to step up in their leadership role of this vital region called the home. Too many young couples act as though both husband and wife are separate free agents with no need for a coordinated center to their lives. This may work for a period of time in the early stages of marriage, but it proves disastrous when kids come along. There must be a leader running the home environment and issues—like a central command unit.

Thankfully, a wife does not have to be the one who personally accomplishes all tasks alone. Her leadership in these areas can, and should be, delegated to and through others. In fact, it is reasonable to divvy up the things that need to get done according to natural ability, time availability, and interests. For example (without sounding too stereotypical), things like household finances (monthly budgets and investments), outdoor maintenance, and indoor repairs could be delegated to the husband while food maintenance, laundry (and other clothing needs), and indoor maintenance could be the wife's domain. It is up to the individual couple to agree on who does what, even down to how the children could be involved as they grow older or if hiring paid help is the answer (providing the financial resources are available).

It doesn't matter how it comes about, but the important point is for a wife to recognize the importance of her role at home and adapt to it as she would any other role she takes on. I remember working with one couple where the husband just sat his wife down and gently said, "I need more leadership from you here in the home. I love you and think it is great to be married to you, but I need you to step up here at home and do more to lead." Thankfully that wife responded to his direct, gentle approach, and began focusing her considerable talents, energy, and leadership for the home and family. Their marriage took a huge step forward as he could rely on her to be a full-fledged teammate and leader with him.

## Marriage Exercise #1

### Casting a Vision

1. In what ways can you as a wife express your leadership to create a warm, inviting home your husband will be drawn to?
2. If you were to assume full responsibility for making the home operate smoothly and the children to grow and develop maximally, how would that change what you do each day?

## A Caution to Working Wives

We read and see in Scripture many gifted women who carried on significant work outside of the home; such as Deborah, Priscilla, Euodia, and Lydia. Indeed, women in the workforce have contributed greatly to our society. A vast number of wives today are college-educated and have much to contribute in terms of their ideas, leadership, and skills. Every wife has a choice to make about how to manage her work and home lives. Some women choose to remain in a full-time career outside of the home for financial reasons, self-fulfillment, and advancement in their careers. Others make the sacrifice to come out of the workforce temporarily, or on a limited basis (part-time), while others quit everything altogether to be home while the children are young.

Maintaining the balance between work and home is especially challenging for working wives in that the home is not the only place where she directs her energy. Her attention is split between two major entities, which means she probably feels pulled in two very different directions. Since working outside the home doesn't eliminate the responsibility of managing the household, delegation and teamwork from other family members will be vital to maintaining the home. Also, she may need to consider lowering her expectations for herself and others for a season unless help can be hired to offset some of the workload.

One Scripture comes to mind when I think on this topic—"If a house is divided against itself, that house will not be able to stand" (Mark. 3:25). If both spouses in the marriage are not fully on board with the working arrangement of the wife, the marriage will undergo major conflict and stress. We have learned a couple of things about God so far in this book...He values marriage, home, and family. He also has delegated the management of home responsibilities to wives. Since each household is different, it would be wise for couples to evaluate the work situation as it relates to the peace and stability in the home as well as the financial need. Ecclesiastes 3 tells us that there is a time for "every event under heaven." Wives, if things are not going well at home and you can manage financially by making some adjustments to your lifestyle, it might be more profitable in the long run for you to return home for a time. Or, at the very least, find a position that is more flexible or amenable to the family situation (a shorter commute, going part-time, less stressful, and so on). I understand this can be very difficult, but it doesn't have to be a forever thing. Plus you may find that you actually like being home as you begin to experience peace and stability on the home front. Seek God in all of these things and allow Him to help you find the answers.

## Signs and Symptoms of a Needed Change

Not all marriages struggle in this area of domestic leadership but some certainly do. There are definite signs and symptoms that arise if this need is not being met in a husband. If wives do not exercise acceptable levels of domestic leadership, she may notice him making statements similar to these:

*"I work as hard as I can and there is never any money."*

*"I come home and there are always demands. Can't I just get a moment's rest?"*

*"The kids are completely out of control."*

*"What did you do all day?"*

While some of these may seem like unfair statements, they communicate his perception – however true it is, or not. If and when she notices her husband is increasingly absent or has withdrawn from being central to the family, she may want to pause and reflect on this area. The chances are that resentment is building, but he isn't verbalizing it yet.

If this is the case, there is good news. Your leadership in this area can reestablish his interest and draw him back into involvement in the home. Just as a CEO of a conglomerate is drawn to spend more time with business affairs that are well-maintained, growing, and successful, so a man is drawn into involvement and leadership in the home that is successful, orderly, and positive.

In our culture the work of domestic leadership has been denigrated. However, what a wife does in this arena of domestic leadership is of the highest and most crucial importance. Proverbs 14:1 says, "The wise woman builds her house, but the foolish tears it down with her own hands." This Scripture says to us that the work a wife does with the home and family determines the joy or sorrow that the whole family will live with for the rest of their lives. Yes, a dad has a crucial role to play and should engage more than what our society suggests, but wayward children and a home in disarray brings constant sorrow and grief to both husband and wife.

I wish it were easy to convince women today that being a great wife is significant and compelling work. We, as a culture, are paying a heavy price for suggesting that home and family don't need or deserve the focused attention of wives. We suffer through increasing numbers of divorces, kids on drugs, teen pregnancies, and lack of moral structure because there is no solidity to home life. It requires sacrifice, leadership, and training. It requires a daily attention to detail and the management of a myriad of issues, problems, and people.

The hub of the family is the wife and mother who takes her role as domestic leader seriously. It is not by accident that some families are enjoyable to be around and others exude chaos and pain. Different marriages work out what this domestic leadership and management role looks like; but great marriages—even those where the wife works outside the home—have an engaged, active wife who exercises domestic leadership. Domestic leadership does make a difference in husbands, in children, and in society. Don't let anyone persuade you of anything different.

A little disclaimer here: I can hear you saying, "So, he just does nothing and I run the house?" That's not what I'm saying at all. I'm saying that women hold the key to making their home and family great. Wives see the big picture and have the ability to determine what needs to be done so that it actually happens. It is not up to you to do it all, just to step up to the plate to get it in motion. For example, if the house is needing attention, you can: 1) do it yourself, 2) hire a house cleaning service, 3) enlist the kids to certain tasks or chores, or 4) work as a team with your husband to get the house in order. Those things require wives to take initiative and be leaders.

## Marriage Exercise #2

## Evaluating Domestic Leadership in Your Home

1. What does domestic leadership look like for you and your family?

2. Describe unique strengths, weaknesses, personalities, contexts, and vocational choices for both you and your spouse.

3. What areas are you currently in charge of handling? Your spouse? What changes need to be made to make your household run more effectively?

4. How does the household need to change to make it more inviting and welcoming for your husband and your children?

5. What are two projects that you and your husband have always talked about but have failed to start?

6. What are two unfinished projects that you could champion?

7. The three most noticeable areas of domestic leadership are physical look of the home, the behavior of the children, and the finances. In the book, *The Millionaire Mind*, Thomas Stanley and William Danko remark that a consistent common denominator of those who have a million dollars in real assets is a wife who is frugal. In what areas could you be more frugal?

8. How do the children need to grow or change to maximize their potential?

# The Risk of Ignoring This Role

The most significant jobs in any culture are those that directly impact the future. This is why the role of wife and mother has been such an honored place in every nation and culture. She changes the future through her management, nurture, and leadership. The crucial importance of this role has been overlooked and degraded by our culture. We have neglected this leadership role and are now paying a high price for our ignorance. Families are flying apart at the seams with irreparable damage done to children. Right now the American culture has a fifty percent divorce rate – meaning that thousands of women and children are forced into poverty and injustice. I have heard of some wives who have refused to adapt to this role and couldn't accept the idea that it is a crucial need in their husband. As a result, the couples divorced blaming the separation on the husband as being unsupportive or uncooperative at home. Our society can't survive without wives fulfilling this domestic leadership role—it's that important.

Today, cultural gurus are trying to invent new cultural roles for men and women. This is extremely unwise. God's mandates are timeless, and He has given men and women explicit advice about how to minister to the needs of the other person. He has spelled out how to build a stable family structure. He has declared that a society that destroys the foundations of the family cannot long survive. It is true that fitting into God's roles for a marriage is confining and not as liberating as unbridled pursuit of one's selfish desires. But God's roles for marriage and family bring stability, peace, and a bright future to each of us. The wise thing is for women to look again at the biblical mandate to supply domestic leadership.

A new problem that many men and women are running into is the idea that exercising leadership gifts at home is a misuse of skills and talents. Society contends that making a life of real meaning involves making money with your skills. This type of thinking has so permeated our culture that men and women do not want to invest their leadership skills in the home and family. The result is that it leaves men with a huge un-fillable hole in their soul. Don't get me wrong—I am not saying that a woman cannot work outside the home ever. I'm stating that a woman should not work for the sake of making money at the expense of her family's wellbeing. It's the motivation behind "why" she works that should be investigated.

Another major misconception that is permeating our current culture is the idea that the perfect wife is a "kept woman," like a mistress with no serious responsibilities. This is a completely distorted viewpoint that grows out of the flawed nobility mindset. I remember one woman who did not want to exercise any leadership in the home. She wanted her husband to do all the leading, managing, and serving. Her idea of a great life was having others wait on her hand and foot. Her husband was a hard worker making an above-average wage, but he absolutely needed her to exercise leadership at home. She had been raised that women were to be spoiled and should not have to work. What do you think was the prognosis for this marriage?

We need to return again to the fully developed understanding of the crucial role that a wife and mother plays in the life of the society. Her actions can make the difference between a stable society and one that crumbles from within. Until wives embrace their role of domestic leadership in the home and society chooses to value this role again, our culture will produce more and more damaged children, marital instability, violence, teen pregnancy, drug use, and the like.

## Undoing the Damage

I have been asked repeatedly by wives, "What will cause my husband to be drawn into an intimate relationship with me?" One of the key answers is to produce a home environment that is orderly, peaceful, welcoming, and safe—a home in which he has a respected role and duties to fulfill. A man is drawn to a peaceful, successful environment where he is respected. That's where he wants to be. Those are the people he wants to be with. If, however, he is always presented with problems, difficulties, criticisms, obstacles, and needs, he is disinclined to want to be there. I realize that a wife can and does look at her husband as a problem solver in their marriage and family. But if she is not producing some level of success in terms of the order, peace, and development of the children, he is not likely to be drawn to that part of his life. When the children are under control, the house is inviting, he is valued, and there is relational peace, he is drawn to this place and drawn to his wife and children.

We are constantly saddened by how the male role is being portrayed in movies, television, and commercials. Men are shown to be stupid, incompetent idiots. There are so many scenarios where the mom and kids are sarcastic and demeaning to men. This is another example of how godly women can make a difference in their homes by being different from the culture. Ladies, don't put your husband down in front of others, especially the kids. Be an example of how to show respect. Many wives in bad marriages do not see themselves as significant parts of the answer to out-of-control kids, a disorderly home, unpaid and overdue bills, and/or bitterness, anger, and emotional tension in the marriage. Like this is somehow someone else's issue. However, godly wives do everything they can to solve these problems.

Many of these problems will require her husband's involvement and help; but a number of them can be significantly changed just through her discipline, leadership, and management. There is something irresistible about a wife who grows her leadership and abilities to the point where she can handle almost all of the common problems involved in running the home. She and her husband can plan, share, and move on to the other things in life. Their marriage is clearly built on the shoulders of her efforts at domestic leadership.

One woman I worked with was not raised to see this aspect of the wife's role. She was reared to be a kept woman, dependent on her husband, naïve, and spending freely. She began growing in her ability to handle domestic issues: calling repair people, writing chore lists for the children, acting when the kids crossed the line, initiating discussions with the kids about issues and pressures they were facing, engaging in serious financial management, and helping create and stay within the budgeted figures. She began to make sure that the home was an inviting place, taking the initiative on the problems and issues she was aware of, and acting with decisiveness and growing wisdom. All these growth areas in her domestic leadership made her irresistible to her husband and greatly increased her own sense of value. Their marriage increased significantly on a number of fronts. Her growing domestic leadership enhanced her personally, relationally, and professionally.

## Male and Female Differences

It is important to remember that a woman is not just a wife and not just a mother. Keep in mind she has nine relationships that comprise her life: God, Marriage, Family, Self, Work, Church, Money, Society, and Friends. It is the health of each of these relationships that brings joy and fullness to her life. Too often women have tried to get all of their joy from their marriage, and men have tried to squeeze all their joy from their work. This is a short- sighted scheme. In each of these nine relationships God has given instructions for having a strong and vibrant life. Since the Fall of man and the entrance of sin into God's creation, there have been difficulties, selfishness, and pain in these relationships. So one can never expect, on this side of heaven, to have all their relationships be great at the same time. We are all a work in progress, following hard after God in each relationship, living His way and bringing joy and health to the various aspects of our lives. This book is a description of only the basic needs of a husband in actionable form so a wife can meet those needs. In that way, she will demonstrate her love to her husband, drawing him to her so they both can reach their fullest potential.

I remember working with a woman years ago whom I showed them the R.A.D.I.C.A.L. list of a husband's deepest needs. She looked at the list for a while and then said rather somberly, "I am only meeting one of these needs. No wonder our marriage is not as good as it could be. I wonder why he puts up with me? He has really been giving, and I have not been meeting his needs." Her attitude was such a delight. She stepped up to her responsibilities as a fully engaged wife and increased the strength and enjoyment of her marriage ten-fold. She and her husband had a good marriage, but her focused involvement took it to another level. Her husband thought she was great before only to have this incredible woman emerge as the woman of his dreams. Too often marriages just bump along being *okay* when, with a little bit of work, it could be *fantastic!*

This is a good time to talk about the different views of home and family that often exist between men and women. For many women, home and family are the center of life and the constant focus of attention with the other aspects of life radiating out from this center. For many men, home and family represents one of a number of separate arenas that are a part of his world. There is the work arena, the friends and hobby arena, the political arena, and the home and family arena. Because they are separate, he needs a great leader organizing and running each one so that when he is in a particular arena, it is done well and right. Husbands often think of their wives as executives of this corporation called "marriage and family." He needs a gifted leader/manager to direct the home and family environment as he gives increasing amounts of time to the work arena. This involves her meeting with and directing the children, as well as nurturing and developing them along agreed-upon lines. This involves taking charge of how the home is run and even helping the husband fit into his own ideal home. Many times men want things a certain way, but they get in the way of that type of home being set up—they are too lenient on the children, they don't pick up after themselves, or they don't help in the places where their involvement is crucial.

If a wife is to be a domestic leader in the fullest sense of this term, she will embrace the leadership role and act accordingly. This means that she identifies strengths and weakness in the marriage and family, examines and prepares for threats, and understands the resource base and expected income along with where the money could and should go. She allocates those resources to the various projects that the family is presented with as well as evaluating the opportunities and goals of the family and how best to accomplish those. For instance, Timmy is capable of being a great student, so here is a plan on how to maximize his potential. Suzy is gifted at these areas, so we should invest in her life in these ways. Our children face these temptations, so we should limit these involvements and these friends. In order to stay together and enjoy life as a family, we need to do these things and overcome these threats. A wife's insight into these various leadership decisions facing the family is invaluable to the marriage and family's success. In general, leadership involves three basic arenas:

**Vision:** direction, goals, plans, steps, tasks, identifying threats, and so on

**People**: training, recruitment, managing, and so on

**Resources:** income, management, and giving

If a wife is to become an effective domestic leader, she must be engaged in all three of these activities for her home, marriage, and family. If she abdicates this leadership responsibility, she diminishes the drawing power of her love that brings her husband to her in order to increase his highest potential.

These and other things are all activities that a wise house leader does to bring about the success of any enterprise. Unfortunately, our modern culture has suggested that high-level leadership is only for making money, not making great relationships. However, when a wife realizes that godly relationships are the key to a great life and she exercises her considerable leadership skills toward building a great marriage and family, then significant change will take place.

## The Danger of Too Much Domestic Leadership

It is possible for a wife to enjoy leadership and control to such a great degree that she organizes her husband right out of the picture. If he is not needed or ignored in household decisions, he may float away from the crucial role that he plays in the family life. A wife cannot and should not give into a man's desire for his wife to do everything while he personally has nothing to do at all with the family. It is critical that he stay engaged for the health of the family. A part of her domestic leadership must include making room for his involvement. Examples of this could be deferring to him about where to place the couch or pictures on the walls, allowing him to arrange a bookcase a certain way, or even pick the color of paint for the walls. A healthy marriage and family requires two partners not just one.

### Marriage Exercise #3

### Developing a Plan

1.  What would happen if you really began to lead and manage your home to accomplish your and your husband's definition of success? What activities would you need to give up? What training might you need to pursue?
2.  What would happen if you really began to lead, act, manage, and recruit to bring about success in your kids' lives?
3.  What would happen if you really began to lead, act, manage, and schedule to maximize the success and enjoyment of your marriage?
4.  If you were to give a report to your husband every week about your efforts to improve the state of your marriage, family, and resources, what would you say? Use the following guide:

**Marriage**

Meeting your husband's deepest needs:

*Respect*

*Adaptation*

*Domestic Leadership*

*Intimacy*

*Companionship*

*Attractive Spouse*

*Listener*

Pursuing your husband's soul:

*How will you do that this week?*

Doing the special things that please him:

*What will you do this week to encourage him?*

**Family**

How will you align your expectations with your husband and children?

What are the strengths of the family?

What are the weaknesses of the family?

What does it not do well?

How can you overcome its weaknesses?

What are the threats to the family?

What are the toxic poisons coming at the family?

*Books*

*Music*

*Television*

*Movies*

*Friends*

*Groups*

*Organizations*

*Relatives*

*Neighbors*

How will you combat and protect against these toxins?

What are good trends that you should encourage?

*People*

*Media*

*Groups*

What are the goals of the family?

Where do you want the family to be or have accomplished in ten years?

How can you make that happen?

What are the opportunities for the family?

## Resource Allocation

There are a number of wonderful tools to help in understanding how to manage money more effectively, including *Crown Ministries* by Larry Burkett, *Financial Peace University* by Dave Ramsey, and Ron Blue's Ministry, to name a few.

- What does resource allocation look like this week?
- How much money will the family have this month?
- Where will it be spent?
- Where should it be spent?

## Marriage Exercise #4

### Aligning Priorities

Aligning expectations between two leaders is crucial to maximize effectiveness. What are the top five things you plan to accomplish this next week, next month, and next year to make the marriage, home, and family successful? What is their order of importance? Make a list for each time frame. See if he agrees. Often a lack of alignment between leaders is the reason behind minimal results and frustration. Ask him what actions he thinks you should take in order of priority and adjust accordingly. Designate who will lead the specified goals.

|            | Marriage                      | Home                          | Family                        |
| ---------- | ----------------------------- | ----------------------------- | ----------------------------- |
| This Week  | 1. <br> 2. <br> 3. <br> 4. <br> 5. | 1. <br> 2. <br> 3. <br> 4. <br> 5. | 1. <br> 2. <br> 3. <br> 4. <br> 5. |
| This Month | 1. <br> 2. <br> 3. <br> 4. <br> 5. | 1. <br> 2. <br> 3. <br> 4. <br> 5. | 1. <br> 2. <br> 3. <br> 4. <br> 5. |
| This Year  | 1. <br> 2. <br> 3. <br> 4. <br> 5. | 1. <br> 2. <br> 3. <br> 4. <br> 5. | 1. <br> 2. <br> 3. <br> 4. <br> 5. |

## Marriage Exercise #5

## Long-Term Planning

What exercises, projects, and changes can a wife do to begin a higher level of domestic leadership? Set time aside to work with your husband to develop a long-term plan. If possible, take some time annually, quarterly, monthly, and weekly to review the plan and make any necessary adjustments along the way. Think in both short-term and long-term time frames so that you'll have clear, measurable goals.

1. If things were to go almost perfectly this next year, what would your home, marriage, and family be like? Is that in line with your husband's goals?

2. What changes can and should be made this next year? What steps need to be taken to get there?

   *Home*

   *Marriage*

   *Family*

      *Child #1*

      *Child #2*

      *Child #3*

      *Child #4*

3. Schedule: What is the ideal week for your family, schedule wise? What needs to change? Describe your ideal morning, afternoon, evening, and weekend. What needs to take place for that to happen?

4. What would our home look and be like if we accomplished the most important projects, cleanups, and maintenance in the next year?

5. What problems exist in this house that I have been waiting for my husband to fix that he may never get to or even notice? Are there any that I can finish?

6. Who do I have to recruit, hire, or invite over to move the home to a level of an acceptable, even pleasant, dwelling place?

7. A successful family involves children who are controlled and well behaved. This training process takes time and effort but is well worth it. Which negative and positive training methods need to be used with our children?

   *Verbal Reprimand*
   *Repetition*
   *Work*
   *Exercises*
   *Rewards*
   *Isolation*
   *Restraint*
   *Chastisement*
   *Removal of Privileges*

8. What would our children act like if we had an enjoyable and successful family? Try to envision it; get a clear picture in your mind:

   *At restaurants*
   *At relatives*
   *At parties*
   *At church*
   *At home*
   *In their rooms*

   What keeps us from already being there?

9.  In ten years, our child (1, 2, 3, 4) will be successful if a, b, or c happened. How do I make a, b, or c happen?

10. Who do I have to recruit, employee, or expose my kids to in order to facilitate the highest possible outcome of their character, ethics, skills, grades, talents, and salvation?

# Chapter 6

## Intimacy

*Genesis 2:24; 1 Corinthians 7:2-5*

They were a young couple with two children and a boatload of troubles. He just would not engage in the marriage or the family; instead, he remained distant. I thought on a number of occasions that their marriage was not going to make it. He wanted to engage with his wife sexually but was largely uninvolved emotionally, mentally, or spiritually. Though she loved him very much, she resisted his constant sexual advances for two reasons: frequency and his hygiene. He worked in construction and would come home smelly and dirty and would not shower until the morning before he went to work. There was constant tension and different expectations in this area. From her point of view, he never wanted to talk and learn about her day or her feelings; he only wanted sex.

I spent hours counseling and working with this couple to stay together and work through their difficulties. It finally clicked in a most unusual way when I made the suggestion to her that if he came home almost every day interested in intimacy, she should use his need as a doorway to explore and meet her need for conversation and involvement. She decided to try the experiment. When her husband came home one day, he opened the front door and found articles of her clothing marking a pathway to the master bedroom and bathroom. She was waiting for him in the shower with the water running. "Want to join me?" she said, peering out of the shower. She wanted to talk with him. You can bet that under these new conditions, he had a new interest in talking with her. He also developed an interest in showering and cleaning up for the evening at home. It was a win-win! By adapting and finding a consistent way to meet his need for physical intimacy, she discovered that she could talk with him about her needs and the needs of the family. When he felt loved consistently and positively in this area, he was energized to meet them. He became a consistent father and a willing participant in their marriage, their spiritual life, and the future as a family. I can only assume that her consistent times to "talk" provided strong and clear motivation and direction for a vibrant, healthy relationship. They are still together, building a good marriage.

## Scriptural Explanation

Let's look at what Scripture says about this issue of intimacy:

*Now concerning the things about which you wrote, it is good for a man not to touch a woman. But because of immoralities, each man is to have his own wife, and each woman is to have her own husband. The husband must fulfill his duty to his wife, and likewise also the wife to her husband. The wife does not have authority over her own body, but the husband does; and likewise also the husband does not have authority over his own body, but the wife does. Stop depriving one another, except by agreement for a time, so that you may devote yourselves to prayer, and come together again so that Satan will not tempt you because of your lack of self-control. (1 Corinthians 7:1-5 NASB)*

It is clear from these passages that men and women need human touch in order to build a good marriage and to keep from surrendering to temptation. Both husbands and wives are in need of physical contact and God has made it clear that it should not be withheld (by either party). Men and women need different kinds of physical contact. Typically, if women were to declare what they need physically from their husbands, it would be tender touch and displays of affection. Men, on the other hand, are physiologically wired to need sexual climax. However, I also know couples where the opposite is true. In general, women have a cycle that moves them to desire sexual climax about once a month. Men have a physiological cycle that moves them to desire sexual climax every two to five days.

That being said, sexual intimacy is one of the most consistent (and sometimes most pressing) needs in a man. It can be described as an almost constant pressure that nags and prods a man toward sex. Since most women do not feel this pressure personally, they believe their husband's constant interest in sex represents some form of deviancy or immorality. This is not true. Your husband has a different physiology that explains his constant orientation in this area.

A typical woman has a physiological need and interest for sexual relations during one time every month that coincides with her highest fertility periods. This process is part of her physiological cycle that takes about a month to complete and produces sexual interest about once or twice during the month. A man, however, has a completely different cycle. Every day a man produces approximately 100-200 million sperm. When he reaches 500 million sperm, he becomes physiologically tuned for sexual intimacy. Therefore, every two to five days he has a physiological need to evacuate this growing number of sperm. When his body reaches this "overproduction" point, he is more heightened to sexual stimulation and sexual involvement. This means that he is physiologically made to be interested in sexual activity every two to five days. This cycle does not slow down until a man reaches his 50s, but it still usually will remain higher than a woman's once-or-twice-a-month cycle. Therefore, if a wife were to wait until she felt like having sexual relations, she would not be meeting her husband's need in this area.[1]

Why did God make men that way? It is quite possible that He put this constant physiological need in men so that they would be constantly drawn back to their wives. A man is never very far from the pull of this need and it causes his mind, emotions, and body to constantly be turned toward home. If home is the place where this relentless need is lovingly and tenderly met in his life, he will be more open to the wisdom, correction, and development that his wife can offer him. He desperately needs the woman he married in this way. Every few days his entire focus is directed toward you to righteously satisfy the longing of his mind, soul, and body. He is tethered to you if he is to live free from guilt.

God designed men to have a natural orientation toward self-sufficiency and world conquering. Think about it! If there were not an internal mechanism that directed him back toward his wife and family, he would mentally, emotionally, and spiritually move away from them seeking his fulfillment, fame, and success completely apart from them. Unfortunately, because of relaxing sexual rules and mores in our society, this is what's happening. Men are finding ways outside of their marriage to satisfy their sexual needs. They are not taught tenderness, faithfulness, and real love through relating to the whole person of their wife. Men who can have their sexual needs met through casual sex with strangers become more selfish, aggressive, and rapacious in all the dealings of their life. The marriage and family suffers the most.

## A Godly Wife's Influence

One of the greatest places a wife can build influence in her family is by meeting his need for physical intimacy in a way that demands a real relationship with the one who provides this need. Without you and the relationship you demand, he will perceive sexual climax as solely about him and as one more way to fulfill his selfish desires. He doesn't necessary know it, but he needs your input, your influence, and your perspective in order to break out of the selfishness that infects him.

It is critical to realize that God has designed your husband to need you sexually every two to five days. Therefore, since women are not typically geared this way, it requires adaptation and surrender on your part. The benefit comes when you meet his need in a caring and compassionate way, moving you into a place of trust and influence. God is counting on you to influence your husband toward his family, faith, and civic duties so that all these places are better because of his involvement. By meeting this need, you are actually contributing to his ability to fulfill his full righteous potential by releasing him from distractions caused by his building sexual tension. It helps him keep his focus, loyalty, and faithfulness to you, the family, and his commitments.

To do this well, a woman needs to figure out her husband's sexual cycle. She most likely will not have the same need for physical intimacy as he does in this area; but if she is to be a godly wife, she needs to embrace his needs as the very definition of what it means to love him. Likewise, he must also seek to understand her needs and meet them even though he may not have those same needs. Just as some men have come to resent their wives' menstrual cycle, so some wives have come to resent their husbands' sexual cycle. Even so, she must understand that meeting his sexual needs helps him reach his full potential as a man.

## Understanding Types of Sexual Intimacy

Almost all great marriages have to work through the timing and style of sexual intimacy. There are three categories: WOW experiences, Normal Experiences, and Quickies. The first sexual category is what I call "WOW" experiences where both husband and wife are interested in sexual activity and fully participating in the passion of it. This usually happens once a month to once every six months. This type of sexual experience is the longest of the types of sexual expression. It can last anywhere from one hour to 2 days from arousal to final climax. This type of sexual expression often involves planning, specific settings, distractions minimized, and passion. In some marriages, this is the only kind of sexual experience that exists in the marriage. While "WOW" sexual experiences are wonderful and a delight to every marriage, the less interested party may come to believe that sexual intimacy is only legitimate with this kind of experience. This is not true. There are other types of sexual experiences that can also be fulfilling and legitimately fulfill this need.

There are a number of factors that control "WOW" experiences: The amount of desire in both individuals (usually one person is more interested than the other); the external pressures on each individual (some people want more sexual expression when they are stressed and other people lose interest in sexual expression when they are under stress); the distractions in the environment that may not allow one of the people to fully release into sexual expression (children, in-laws, noise, apartment neighbors, etc.); the amount and frequency of arguments and disagreements in the marriage that week (you don't stop needing to eat just because you have had a fight, so you don't stop needing to have sexual expression just because you have had a fight).

The second type of sexual expression is called "normal" sexual experiences. This is the beginning of sexual intimacy for the other person. Normal experiences are usually weekly sexual encounters in which the uninterested party can be encouraged to engage in sexual expression and actually enjoy the experience, but they do not desire it initially. For most couples in America this is once a week. This type of sexual expression often lasts between ten minutes to one hour in length from arousal to climax. It is important for the uninterested party (usually the woman, but not always) to realize that they have a partner who is very much interested in sexual expression and/or release, so ministering to their need is more important than whether they feel like it.

In normal sexual expression, one person in the marriage initiates the time of intimacy and the other person (out of respect and love for the other person) schedules or takes the time to engage with their spouse in sexual intimacy. I have often asked women if they would do something mildly enjoyable 30 minutes once a week in order to keep their husband from straying into the arms of another woman. Many have not thought of sexual intimacy in this way. Many are still thinking back in a dating mentality about sexual intimacy ("But I am not interested." "Doesn't he have to make me interested?"). In order to keep your marriage strong and growing, there are times when you will need to minister to his needs even though it may not be as enjoyable to you as it is for him.

For many husbands and some wives, occasional "WOW" encounters and regular "normal" encounters are not enough to meet their needs for sexual expression. If this is the case, then a third category is added – "quickies." These types of sexual encounters occur when one party is stimulated and the other party is less stimulated or not sexually engaged at all. There are innumerable ways to accomplish this level of sexual intimacy, but two consistent elements are that it usually takes less than ten minutes from arousal to climax, and it usually does not involve both parties climaxing sexually.

## Risks of Not Meeting the Need

We realize this can be a difficult commitment for some wives, but there are great risks involved when this need in a man goes unmet. If a man is allowed or driven to meet his sexual needs outside of the marriage bond, it will twist his understanding of women and harden his conscience to the kindness he needs to be able to display to his wife and family.

When a wife understands her husband's sexual cycle and meets his needs intimately, it helps him avoid the ravages of anonymous sex and pornography. Unfortunately, a man will often turn to pornography to try and meet his own sexual needs; but this tends to increase his appetite, not satisfy it. A man exposed to pornography on a regular basis will have an increased appetite for sexual activities, which oftentimes leads to twisted activities he would have never thought of on his own. This is why the availability of pornography and sexually-charged media is so damaging to a healthy marriage relationship. A man who is having his sexual needs met in marriage has a greater ability to resist the temptation of pornography.

Sexual intimacy must be fulfilled and understood as a "knowing" of the other person, not just as a satisfying of lust. This happens within the context of a relationship with a real person (his wife). I have found that if a man "needs" sexual intimacy more often than every two to five days, he is usually exposed to pornography. Addiction to pornography is prevalent in society today and is extremely toxic to marriages. No real person can live up to the fantasies and pornographic images on display, and so a man's desire for his own wife decreases. Either that or he may try to get her to go beyond what she is comfortable with.

According to the American Academy of Matrimonial Lawyers, Internet pornography and sex addiction are significant factors in two out of three divorces.[2] Biblically, the viewing of pornography is equivalent to adultery. In Matthew 5:27-30, Jesus defines an adulterer as "anyone who looks at a woman with lust for her." Why? Because it breaks the marriage bond and defiles the trust between the married couple. A wife has a role to play in keeping her husband away from this toxic, harmful activity. How? She figures out his sexual cycle and meets him there, even when she may not want to.

Sadly, there are, in certain circles, the idea that a wife should allow her husband to delegate his sexual needs to mistresses and one-night stands so that he is satisfied and less demanding of his wife. However, this promotes all kinds of evil. It spreads disease, unfaithfulness, lack of discipline, selfishness, guilt, unwanted pregnancy, rape, victimization, oppression, and so on. A healthy marriage involves a real relationship between a husband and a wife in all areas of life. Sexuality is not a delegable task.

## Dealing With a Wife's Sexual Self-Image

A woman's self-image can oftentimes get in the way of desiring sexual intimacy. She may not feel sexy enough in her own eyes to match the desire that her husband expresses toward her. Subconsciously, it's almost like she doesn't understand why he would find her attractive at all and has a hard time accepting any compliments about her body as truth. She knows what she sees in the mirror when she looks at herself, so he must be just saying those nice things to get what he wants, right? Well, let me share with you an amazing mystery of how God designed a man to have only eyes for his wife. This, of course, is provided that he isn't engaged in pornography or other illicit activities where he might be tainted.

When a man feels attracted to his wife and wants to be intimate with her, he is not focused on every detail of her body or what she looks like at the moment (even though she might be). When he looks at her, he sees her beauty in all her femininity and curves. He loves her and needs her. The body she has makes him happy and he sees it as God's gift for him. For a woman to understand this point, it is important to see his needs as unique and different from hers; also, it helps to understand that male brains are hard-wired to see beauty in the female body. In other words, his definition of what he finds beautiful may be different from her definition of what is beautiful.

The mystery of God lies in the fact that a man finds his wife even more beautiful and attractive as she grows older, which is contrary to what women believe. Women are constantly trying to go back in time—to make their bodies look young again—because to her that's the time when she felt most beautiful. But the interesting thing is that he doesn't need her to do that. If he is a man free from outside influences, he will naturally find her body beautiful just as it is and will continue to do so as they age together. Now this doesn't mean women (or men) have to stop trying to take care of their bodies. As believers in Christ, our bodies are God's temple, holy and set apart (1 Corinthians 3:16). We will cover this subject in much more depth in Chapter 8.

140

Meeting his needs in the sexual arena may not be an exciting, passionate exchange at all times but realize that you are loving him and meeting a need that has the power to bring the two of you close.

## Loving First as a Godly Strategy

What many women have a hard time understanding is that a man's incredibly strong and relentless need for sexual intimacy is normal, even though it is so different from hers. It's easy to think that your husband is being weird or selfish in this area but he truly has a need; and he wants his wife to be close, connected, and loving with him. It might be helpful to think of his sexual need in a couple of ways. Let me paint a couple of word pictures for you to broaden your understanding:

- You could equate his sexual need to a headache that starts small and increases in pain and intensity over time. Imagine if you had a headache that reoccurs every two to five days. As time continues, your ability to function in everyday life diminishes bit-by-bit. Your attitude is affected; you become irritable, edgy, and unfocused. The bulk of your thoughts become more about how to get rid of the headache than anything else. The choices are limited; you need a pain reliever. Relating to our topic on intimacy, as a wife, you are your husband's pain reliever.

- From a mother's point of view, think about how annoying or distracting it is when you have a child that won't stop talking or crying or worse—they try to get your attention by poking you! You are trying to concentrate on the task at hand or attempting to have an adult conversation with a friend, but one or more of your children interrupts. They need your attention! It begins subtly at first:

*"Mommy…(poke)…mommy…(poke)…mommy…(poke)."*

But, as you continue to go on with what you were doing, trying to concentrate or focus, the interruption continues—

*"Mommy…(poke, poke)…Mommy…(poke, poke, poke)…"*

Imagine it continues like this for two to five days until the whining and crying and poking is so intense, you finally give in and turn your attention toward them. The only way to get rid of the annoying poke is to take care of the need. As it relates to the topic of intimacy, this refers to a husband's sexual release with his wife. He looks to you first to eliminate the need for him.

Like a headache or an annoying poke, a man has a hard time focusing on the other aspects of his marriage, family, and life because this need is screaming at him. *The only person in the whole world who can meet his sexual need without guilt is his wife.* What happens if she doesn't do this for him? He concludes that she does not love him or that he is defective in some way. He can even experience her *no's* as an utter and complete rejection of him as a man if it happens too many times in a row. Men also tend to believe that their wives have the same needs that they do, and therefore she must be holding out, is sick, or somehow displeased with him.

Since men are natural problem solvers, and they have this problem that needs to be solved. They go into a "fix it" mode on their own. The very last thing you want your husband to do is to ask on his own, "I have this problem (need). What should I do to fix it?" Ladies, you want to be his fixer. The reality is that when men are left to fix the problem themselves, it can lead to much

142

more than you ever realized—pornography, masturbation, addiction, affairs, pain, guilt, and so on.

Loving him first is a godly strategy that wives can employ. It involves knowing his sexual cycle and understanding his individual need. Just as a woman is not drawn to her husband unless he is giving her honor, understanding, and affection, a man is not drawn toward his wife if his number one need is not being met. If we demand that the other person love us first before we will love them, usually we have a stand off with both parties waiting. This typical "you-first" orientation in marriage really says, "I will love you if you earn my love." This turns marriage into a business arrangement and destroys the ability of deep intimacy. On the other hand, either spouse may say, "I choose to meet the needs of my spouse, to love them and fill them up. I understand that God will take my case and my needs when I have filled them with my love." This approach of choosing to lavish your love upon your spouse first builds intimacy and trust.

When couples begin meeting the needs of their spouse, they are being loving, even when those particular needs are not the same as their needs. When we meet the needs of our spouse, they are then more naturally inclined to meet our needs. They can be lovingly directed and trained to return love to us. Some people are shocked that I would suggest a wife use her husband's need for physical intimacy as a tool to explain her needs or to accomplish the needs of the family. But this is how a good relationship works. A wife meets the needs of her husband and, at some point, uses his love to leverage a conversation about her unique needs. When a conversation takes place within the context of love and care, both partners explain their needs and how the other person can meet them.

Let me give you an example. A few women I knew needed their husbands to be more affectionate and less sarcastic. They decided to put my "strategy" to the test. They agreed to consistently meet their husband's sexual needs for a period of time, monitoring his sexual cycle and loving him first. Then they began to suggest specific ways they needed more affection and areas of sarcasm that needed to be reduced. In each case, these requests were met with immediate change because of the context of love that surrounded the request. This was not meant to be manipulative or devious; it is the way mutual relationships work. It is really saying, "I will meet your needs, and since you are filled up by my love, I will guide you into learning how to love me more effectively." A mutually satisfying relationship in any area of life means both parties are getting what they want and need. This mutual giving and receiving is what keeps people in the relationship.

I have heard people complain, "I shouldn't have to tell my husband/wife how to meet my needs; they should just know if they truly loved me." This is a romance movie myth. People need to learn and grow in their ability to meet each other's needs. Consistent back-and-forth communication is crucial to a satisfying relationship. Mutually satisfying relationships start by one party giving more and then helping the other party "catch up." When one side of what is supposed to be mutual relationship consistently is under-loved, then it puts a strain on the relationship. Eventually, the one-sided relationship will break down. Therefore, it is imperative that husbands and wives understand how to meet the needs of the other.

I have watched couples have helpful, positive conversations about their needs and how to resolve the differences. Marriages begin to heal when one or both parties commit themselves to meeting the real needs of their spouse and then communicating gently and positively what their needs are. If we want our marriages to become a deep and lasting friendship, it involves a mutual agreement between two people that they will meet each other's needs. Those needs are different in a woman than in a man. That is why God commands a man to do different things for his wife than He commands for a woman to do for her husband.

The top seven needs of a man are to be met by the woman and having met them, she can gently and lovingly interact with him about meeting her needs. Intimacy is a huge need that contributes greatly to this goal when met. When there is a mutual flow of needs between the two parties, then a depth of friendship between the two is possible. It is not possible if one or both sides are holding out on meeting the other's needs.

There was one couple I knew that should have had a terrible marriage but because of the wisdom of the wife, they developed a great marriage. We will call her Jessica. She was a vivacious woman, full of life. What struck you on meeting her was how bright and cheerful she was. Her husband, who was rather shy, was always in a good mood and was clearly performing above his potential. She obviously had more energy and drive than her husband.

I had seen this type of marriage many times in counseling. Usually in this kind of marriage, I would hear the wife complaining about how her husband would not talk to her, how he was withdrawn and lazy, and how he was not living up to his potential. But I never saw this lady or her husband in counseling. They never needed my help. In fact, they were full of practical and wise advice to other married couples on how to have a vibrant marriage. What was the secret to her full life and her deeply enjoyable marriage?

She took it upon herself to meet her husband's needs. She studied him and acted accordingly. In fact, she might be a better person to write this book! In this area of intimacy, she was a master of meeting her husband's need. I am quite sure that she never had formalized classes on how to meet them, but she guided her husband through her love for him about how to skillfully love her to the depth of her being. She used his needs as springboards and doorways to the development of a great marriage. He was one deeply grateful man.

Ladies, never forget that a man has a deep and lasting need for sexual intimacy, and he will adjust and grow and change in order to keep this need met. It is the wise woman who "without a word" brings her husband to the place where he knows how to meet her needs.

## Marriage Exercise #1

### Determining His Sexual Cycle

The first step in meeting his sexual need is determining his individual sexual cycle. There are several signs and symptoms to watch for, including increases in: his need to touch you, his attraction to you, your beauty in his mind, his interest and notice of women in general, and his temptation to pornography. Often a man will have a backlogged interest in sex that may not allow you to read it correctly at first. What is your husband's sexual cycle based on these clues?

*Every other day*
*Every third day*
*Every fourth day*
*Every fifth day*
*Every sixth day*

*Every seventh day*
*Twice a month*
*Once a month*

## Marriage Exercise #2

### Sexual Intimacy Considerations

Because you are looking at a lifetime of meeting your husband's completely different sexual needs, some pre-planning allows you to survive and even thrive. Thinking through each area allows a whole new level of encouragement in this consistent reality of marriage. Be creative with your answers!

1. Think through the following categories to bring about a lifetime of fulfilling sexual encounters. It can be very helpful if one or both of the partners has an idea of how the sexual encounter will progress.

   *What lead-in (foreplay) will you use?* Matter of fact, date, weekend, scenarios, flirting, massage, talking, shopping, long walk, touches, other?
   *What setting will you use?* Master bedroom, other places in the house, hotel, outdoors, other?
   *What position(s) will you use?* Man on top, woman on top, side-by-side, other?
   *What method(s) will you use?* Intercourse, mutual stimulation, one-way stimulation, role-play, other?

2. How long does it usually take for your husband to reach climax? Is this an area to help him work on?
   *5 minutes*
   *10 minutes*
   *15 minutes*

*30 minutes*
*60 minutes*

3. What is your husband's preferred method of sexual fulfillment? Notice I did not ask what his sexual fantasies are. There is often an assumption on a woman's part that what the couple is currently doing sexually is his preferred method. But men enjoy variety. If possible, have a discussion with your husband about this area. Is he open to trying other methods of meeting his need for sexual fulfillment? What are they?

*Preferred Method #1*
*Preferred Method #2*
*Preferred Method #3*

## When Loving First Doesn't Work

What I have observed in looking at good, bad, and ugly marriages for years is that the good ones usually have this area of sexual intimacy tuned up. It is such a huge need in men that without this being met, it is just not possible to have a really good marriage. I have met many "Jessica's" and the interesting thing is that they usually have good marriages. However, this does not always mean that those with a healthy and vibrant sex life have a great marriage. There are other issues at play.

There are about 20 to 30 percent of wives who will have more potential interest in sexual intimacy than their husbands. These women want to please their husbands sexually, but the husband is the one saying *no.* They can probably relate to feelings of rejection and feeling unloved that some of the text in this chapter describes. It might help for her to understand the possible factors involved in why the situation is the way it is. Possibilities include low testosterone on the husband's part (or higher testosterone on the

148

wife's part), his temperament, the demeanor or attitude of the wife (possible lack of respect), unrealistic expectations of either the husband or the wife, the lack of pleasure in the act itself by the husband, previous wounds in the sexual arena, erectile dysfunction in the past or present, the level of stress in the husband's life, and a hundred other possible things.

No matter what the sexual inequalities are – whether they exist on the male or female side – there are some basic ground rules that help. First, communicate what your needs are for "WOW," "normal," and "quickie" sex. Second, communicate the frequency of your desire for sexual activity. Third, help him get to the root of the issue, guiding him to come out of a self-focused point of view so he can minister to your needs, even if he is not all that interested. God is asking women to do this; and, therefore, that same commandment extends to men. Remember 1 Corinthians 7:1-5? It can be helpful to understand where the inequity is coming from, but a couple must talk and walk through what they need to do in order to meet each other's needs even if their marriage does not fit the norm.

Other factors that can hinder a healthy sex life in marriage is the fact that some people have been so emotionally or psychologically damaged by wounds, trauma, and destructive events in their life that they have little, if any, ability to ever reciprocate love. These people just take and take and take. Until they walk through a process of dealing with their pain, grief, and trauma, they will not automatically or easily respond to "now-its-your-turn-to-love-me." But when you meet their needs, you bring them to an intermediate step in which they have a new energy or willingness to process their pain. It is the processing of their pain, grief, and trauma that will eventually allow them to love responsively and genuinely.

The difficulty with this is that it feels like another selfish "I-want-you-to-meet-my-needs" agenda. When their deepest needs are met, it gives them energy to want you to listen and help them process their pain. At this point, a counselor or professional may be needed as it may become too draining for a spouse to be everything for their needy mate.

There are a segment of people who do not want to overcome their pain, grief, or trauma. They want to be emotional leeches, sucking people dry and never giving. This kind of person will drain you and then move on to someone else. So deal with them lovingly but also with strong, and at times, restrictive emotional, physical, mental, and spiritual boundaries. Even in these cases, Jesus gave loving admonition for them to control their raging selfishness. You love them by pointing out this need and refusing to meet their selfish demands unless they are willing to grow through processing their grief, pain, loss, and problems.

## Meeting This Need in Everyday Life

Godly wives realize that their husbands have this need, will have this need every few days, and will embrace this half-hour to one-hour responsibility with gusto and energy. While it is often true that she is not personally interested in intimacy every few days, she makes a conscious decision to meet her husband's need on an on-going basis. She gears up for this time with vigorous energy, much like she would when she is expecting guests or serving others. She schedules the time just as she would the laundry, dinner, or piano lessons for the kids. She develops multiple ways of meeting her husband's need for sexual intimacy—some are quick, while some are lengthy; some take significant planning, while some are very spontaneous; some are aggressive, while some are passive.

Since it is a reoccurring event and it involves a person of high priority, it is something that takes priority over other action items to see that it gets done. She does not wait until the mood strikes her or when she feels like it. She is engaged in the sexual experience to meet his need, not her own. However, when she is interested (usually once or twice a month), her husband gets a bonus. She will say that even though she is not interested personally, once she is involved, sexual intimacy is actually pleasant and enjoyable. She knows that her husband is getting more out of this time than she is—just as her husband sits and actively engages in conversation with her and realizes that she is getting far more out of that time than he is. It involves a sacrifice—not just of time, but her whole being—a letting go, you might say.

Too often men and women have embraced the ridiculous idea that they will only do something when they feel like it. There are all kinds of things that one does just because they need to be done. To rely on an inner desire to tell you when to meet another person's need is being lazy and self-centered. This is not the way that strong relationships are built. We would never think this way at work; if we did, we would surely find ourselves unemployed.

This line of reasoning would never work with raising children, either, would it? What if we only fed our children when we felt like it? What if we only sent them to school when we felt like getting up and getting them ready? We feed our children when they need to eat, even though the process of getting the food and preparing it is inconvenient and time-consuming. They need it, so we do it. We send our children to school and educate them because they need it, not because we like getting up early, making lunches, or preparing breakfast.

During courtship and dating, both partners feel like meeting the needs of the other person. This is the conquering/alluring process. Men are interested in conversing with their wives and romancing them; women are interested in sports and sex. It is a part of the wonder of attraction. But once you get married, the things that were easy during dating now become the job description of a marriage.

Meeting the needs of your spouse is the way you build a great relationship. A great relationship is based upon both husbands and wives meeting each other's needs; therefore, being bonded to this person through whom these deep, personal, and intimate needs are met is the secret to not be looking for someone else to meet these needs. The wise woman realizes that she has the opportunity to train her husband how to meet her deepest needs. He will keep coming to her to have his needs met if she always meets them. She can wisely orient him to her needs through her strong and consistent love for him.

## Marriage Exercise #3

## Planning For Sexual Intimacy

How will you prepare and plan to meet his intimacy needs? As with most recurring items in your schedule, if you plan and prepare for them, it works out better than if one is constantly surprised by regular occurring items. We must resist the idea that planning sexual intimacy lowers the romantic value—"If it is really romantic, it will be spontaneous." No, if you really love another person, you will spend time thinking of ways for you to meet their needs. Begin by answering the following questions about your husband's sexual need for intimacy this week:

*When will he need it?*

*What days will you meet his sexual need this week?*
*What kind of sex will he need (WOW, normal, or quickie)?*
*How will you meet his need for sexual intimacy this week?*
*How much time do you need to allot in your schedule to meet his need?*
*Where will you meet his sexual need this week?*
*What preparations need to be made to ensure a positive time of sexual intimacy?*

## Educating Your Husband

In most cases there is a need for a wife to educate her husband about what pleases her sexually. He desperately wants to be considered a good lover and will not necessarily know how to do this unless she helps him (especially at the beginning of the marriage). Many men think they already know how to please their wives through what they have heard or seen in pornographic depictions. These "truths" are often what your husband is basing his sexual actions upon. He needs his wife to make sure that he has accurate information to become a great lover for her. He may need to be guided during the sexual experience itself so that the experience is the most pleasurable for both partners. How does a wife educate her husband about what pleases her? Let me suggest four keys to a husband's receptivity to new information in the sexual arena.

1.  The new information needs to be positive, not negative. ("I love when you do this." Move his hands the way you would like, and so on.) In other words, you should not be critical of what he is doing, but suggest some new things you might be interested in having him try.

153

2. It can be most helpful if new ideas are discussed as an experiment or something to try.

3. New ideas should be shared before he has climaxed. A man is the most interested in his wife during the build-up to sexual climax; therefore, if foreplay can be lengthened to include new experiments, it has his attention. Some men have not trained themselves to move slowly enough through the build-up process, and this could be another aspect of sexual discovery and learning. If a man can control his climax, he heightens his sexual pleasure and his ability to give and receive pleasure during the time of intimacy.

There are a number of Christian and secular books that show husbands and wives how to slow down his race to climax so that maximum foreplay and enjoyment for both parties can be achieved. Growth in this area often involves the loving assistance of a patient wife. A man should be able to understand and control himself sexually so that he can climax in five minutes or one hour.

4. It is best if your husband has climaxed a number of times in the days or week before you share new information. Then he won't be as pent up, and it will be easier for him to slow down his drive to climax.

### Marriage Exercise #4

### Educating Your Husband Sexually

Sometimes it is necessary to educating your husband about what pleases you sexually. This process is not always easy or straightforward, but it is important. The following questions will make you list out some of the needed changes in your sexual encounters. This is not a list of demands but instead a series of goals to begin moving toward. If your relationship with your husband is very open and able to handle discussions about this intimate area, you may want to reverse these questions and have your husband answer the questions about what he would like (or not like) from you in each of the phases of physical intimacy.

*What are five things that you would like your husband to do to warm you up before a sexual encounter?*

*What are five things you want your husband to stop doing as he leads up to a sexual encounter?*

*What are five things that you would like your husband to add to your sexual encounters? You might want to look at each of the five senses to help you get started: sight, sound, touch, smell, and taste.*

*What are five things you would like your husband to stop doing in your sexual encounters? Look again at the five senses as a way of jump-starting your thinking: sight, sound, touch, smell, and taste.*

*What are five things you don't know about sexual intimacy that you would like to know?*

*What are five things that you would like your husband to do after your sexual encounter is over?*

*What are five things that you would like your husband to stop doing after your sexual encounter is over?*

## Marriage Exercise #5

### Variety in Sexual Intimacy

What are ten different, righteous means of bringing sexual fulfillment to you and your husband? This would include different positions, different settings, different times, different lead-ins, and so on. As a wife, your planning, creativity, understanding, and initiation in this area will be crucial to meeting this need in your husband. This is also a project that your husband would probably enjoy participating in.

1.

2.

3.

4.

5.

6.

7.

8.

9.

10.

## Problems Within Sexual Intimacy

This book is not a detailed sexual manual, but there can be problems in sexual relations within marriage. Sometimes these problems are complex and time consuming and may require the help of a counselor, pastor, or trained professional. Realize that resolving some of these issues may take a lot of time, but that also there are solutions and help if these issues are handled with love and openness in the family. In this section we will talk about six common problems in sexual intimacy.

**Premature Ejaculation.** This is the problem of a husband's quick, uncontrolled climax. There is no time for him to really feel the build-up of intimacy and enjoy the time of sharing, touching, and loving before he climaxes. An inability to slow down the climax does not allow his wife time to warm up. He has already climaxed and is losing interest; she is left feeling used and unfulfilled.

A number of good Christian books discuss this problem in detail with ways to slow down a husband's ejaculation so that he may pleasure his wife and enjoy intimacy on a whole new level. Helping a husband to new levels of control in this area will take the patient involvement of his wife. They should be seeking to develop his ability to hold an erection for between twenty minutes and one hour without climax.

**Impotence.** Impotency is the inability of a man to obtain or maintain an erection during sexual excitement until he reaches sexual climax. This problem affects men of all ages. Many men see this as a personal manhood issue; and it can bring on depression, distance, and even divorce. A man's ability to achieve sexual climax is often so personally woven into his self-concept that an inability in this area for any reason can be crushing. Impotence can be physical as well as psychological, emotional, and spiritual. It often occurs because of a combination of physical exhaustion and stress. A faithful, supportive, and encouraging wife is crucial to a man as he works through the issues that may be at the root of this problem. There are a host of pills that are on the market to help men obtain and maintain the potency to achieve sexual climax. He should talk to his doctor first before trying anything.

**Anger.** A man's need for sexual release in marriage does not take a holiday if the couple is fighting or arguing. At times, this can lead to a huge disconnect between his interest in sexual relations with his wife and the general state of their marriage. There is a need to know how to resolve anger and disagreements in marriage. If too much anger is allowed to build up in a marriage, the husband can use his anger or size to demand sexual release or the wife can close off the sexual arena completely to her husband since she does not feel like it. A man is completely capable of saying hurtful things, yelling, and creating great fear and then in an hour want physical intimacy. Many marriages need to address the issue of unresolved anger and bitterness. Anger is a question of unmet expectations. Until the issue of unmet expectations is dealt with, there will be no resolution to the anger issues. Bitterness is an issue of hurts, wounds, and forgiveness. Until confession, mercy, and forgiveness are common aspects of a marriage, this will continue to be a problem.

**Deviancy.** As our culture becomes more post-Christian, men and women are exposed to all types and styles of sexual expression. Much of this is clearly not how the body was meant to perform. These perversions of normal bodily functions usually do physical, emotional, and psychological—as well as spiritual—harm to the individuals as well as the couple. Partners in a Christian marriage should not be involved in perversions of sexuality. This would include any action that harms, hurts, degrades, shames, tortures, or wounds the other person's body, mind, soul, or conscience.

The wonder of marital sexual love is to be a place of intimacy, not seeking selfish pleasure with little thought to the soul or body of the other. A wife should meet her husband's need for physical intimacy, but she should not participate in perversions of sexual intimacy. Sexual fulfillment should be abundant and intimate within marriage, but sexual perversions that degrade the personhood and, at times, wound the soul of the person should not be permitted. She could lovingly say, "Honey, I love you, but I will not do that!" A woman cannot and should not give into a man's desire to participate in sin, perversion, or wickedness. Every attempt should be made to keep the marriage honorable and the marriage bed undefiled (Hebrews 13:4).

**Education.** Knowing how the other spouse thinks, feels, and functions in the sexual arena is one of the key problems in marital sexuality. Does a wife really understand how her husband feels about physical intimacy? Does she understand how her body and his body really function together during this act of intimacy? Does she really understand his need for this expression of love? Does he understand how to make love tenderly? Does he understand that she does not have the same need that he does? Does he want to learn how to please her in the sexual process?

One of the most difficult but rewarding areas to discuss openly is one's sexual needs and desires. There is often a need for open communication and new information in this area of life. Many of the exercises in this book are designed to be a way to broach this subject in a non-threatening and educational way.

**Pornography.** With the rise of pornography in the last forty years, our culture (and men in general) has been stirred up in the sexual arena in all kinds of deviant ways. There is no righteous way to fulfill all the desires and ideas that pornography stirs up in a man. If a man makes a regular habit of viewing pornography, this stirring up of his sexual passions will show up in his daily life, in his conscience, and in his sexual relations with his wife. Pornography is becoming an increasingly big problem in our society and is now considered to be an addiction, much like alcohol and drugs. As the images and ideas of vile behavior seep into men's minds, they begin to view them as normal. This causes some men to make increasing bizarre requests of their wives to behave like the women in the magazines or videos. There are excellent books available for men caught in this trap; for example, *An Affair of the Mind,* by Laurie Hall, *Every Man's Battle,* by Stephen Arterburn, and, *Mission Possible: Winning the Battle over Temptation,* by Gil Stieglitz.

## Marriage Exercise #6

## Boundaries to Intimacy

A woman should not get involved in sexual pleasure or fulfillment that is degrading, violates his conscience, hurts, or does violence to her or her husband. Instead, she should gently direct her husband's needs to be met through righteous and varied involvements of a married couple. There are many sexual perversions that destroy a person's self-worth. Sexual fulfillment should never involve these practices. A few rules to go by:

**Teach him your parameters for healthy sexuality.**

If there are potentially some things that your husband wants you to do sexually that you are uncomfortable about or adamant in your opposition of, this needs to be communicated gently and respectfully.

**That which is unhealthy or uncomfortable should be avoided.**

Because of the openness of pornography and aberrant sexuality, many men may have had exposure to sexual practices that are unhealthy or perverted. A wife should communicate clearly

160

regarding what she is unwilling to do in the context of actually meeting his physiological need for sexual release and intimacy.

**The following should be considered unhealthy or aberrant desires:**

*Sodomy*
*Multiple partners*
*Bondage rituals*
*Spiritual rituals*
*Beastiality*
*Hitting, wounding, or hurting*
*Pornography*

### Marital Exercise #7

### Understanding Intimacy

It is essential that a wife begin to be knowledgeable about this need in her husband. The more understanding that she has about how to meet this need, how to overcome sexual problems, and how to bring vitality and freshness to this area, the more effective she will be in meeting this most important need in her husband. Read a book or listen to a tape from a Christian author that details lovemaking within marriage. Some recommendations are:

*Intended for Pleasure,* by Ed Wheat and Gaye Wheat
*The Act of Marriage,* by Tim and Beverly LaHaye
*Sexual Intimacy in Marriage,* by William Cutrer, MD, and Sandra Glahn
Do a Bible study on the *Song of Songs*
*Return to the Garden: Embracing God's Design for Sexuality,* by Kay Arthur

## Four Ways a Husband Needs You Intimately

A husband has a complex need in this arena of sexual intimacy. It is a relentless need; but it is also requires intimacy, not just the release itself. In other words, there are huge aspects of his being that are wrapped up in meeting this need for physical intimacy. In this section, I will outline four ways your husband needs you to meet this need for sexual intimacy.

### He Needs You To Want Him Sexually

A key component for telling him that you love him is through sexual relations. If you want to say to him, "I love you," initiate sex with him. This says, "I love you" in ways few things do. At some level, it is a serious affirmation of him as a person that his wife wants to have sex with him without his having to initiate it. This tells him that he has qualities, talents, abilities, and substance enough to be a wanted person. On the other hand, if a wife wants to reject a man or tell him that she doesn't love him or that she doesn't care for him, then on-going refusal to have sex with him relays that message loud and clear. When a woman never brings up a desire to have sex with her husband, he often takes that as a sign that she does not love him. Men tend to believe that women think and feel like they do. So they tend to believe that if they are the only ones who ever initiate sex, then they are the only ones who are in love in this relationship. In his mind, he thinks, *If she loved me, she would want me. So, since she doesn't want me... ever... (I always have to initiate sex), she does not really love me.* This is not the way a woman thinks, but it is the way a man thinks.

A man needs a woman to initiate, desire, and want sexual relations from him in order to communicate that she loves him. He needs to be reassured from time to time that she still wants him, that she loves him. At times it is hard for a woman to separate the difficulties in the marriage from the good things about her husband. She wants all of these difficulties resolved before she can focus on his good points.

Many of the sexual fantasies of men involve a woman who wants him and expresses that want in a sexual way. In his mind this is the best way of saying, "I find you fascinating, stimulating, important, beautiful, interesting, successful, significant, desirable." For this kind of woman he is willing to change, grow, and develop. Remember, ladies, this is the way his mind works. You don't have to agree with how it works, just understand how it works and use that communication method.

The next time there is a big decision to make or you know of a stressful situation coming up that will require cooperation between you and your husband, try this—anticipate the need and initiate intimacy with your husband beforehand. You'll be surprised at how much better the two of you work together and how much less tension there is between you. It puts both of you on the same page and on each other's side. This is also helpful:

- *The night before leaving for a big vacation or fast-paced trip.*
- *Before a visit from out-of-town guests, like your parents or in-laws.*
- *Before beginning major renovations (and during).*
- *Before leaving for a business trip for either of you.*
- *Before going to an important meeting for work.*
- *Before you are due to receive some important news.*

## Marriage Exercise #8

### Initiating Intimacy

What is your husband's response to your initiating sexual interest and/or fulfillment—positive or negative?

What range of sexual initiation is your husband expecting and encouraged by?

*Feigning disinterest*
*Dressing up, dressing down, dressing "sexy"*
*Unusual attire*
*Flirting*
*Verbal hints*
*Sexual stare*
*Spoken requests*
*Touch*
*Kiss*
*Sensual kiss*
*Verbal scenarios*
*Undressing*
*Sexual touch*

**He Needs You to Want And Enjoy Physical Intimacy Yourself**
All of us are drawn to those who like and enjoy the things we do. In his mind sexual relations is one of the best and most enjoyable things to do in the whole world. It seems strange that his wife is not interested in this "Shangri-La." Some women have, in a number of ways, internalized a dislike or abhorrence to the sexual experience. This is unfortunate and often needs to be worked through because of this area's importance in a man's life.

While many women do not desire sexual intimacy as much as a man, he needs to know that once she is in the experience, it is a pleasurable time for her. If it causes physical, emotional, or psychological pain, he feels guilty for needing and wanting something that disturbs and distresses his wife so much. It is in this area where a wife should learn about how to enjoy the sexual encounters, how to guide him to improve her physical intimacy, and how to overcome whatever bad associations this way of expressing love has become laden with. We have included a number of exercises that will help in healing this area. If either of you need to see a counselor, pastor, or therapist regarding past victimizations in this area, then take that step. We recommend *The Invisible Bond: How to Break Free from Your Sexual Past* by Barbara Wilson. This is a good resource for helping to heal past sexual sins.

A woman needs to communicate how she wants to be pleased sexually and that she enjoys sex within those parameters. A man tends to rate himself as a husband based on his ability to satisfy his wife in this crucial area. If he cannot satisfy her, he may feel like a failure and believe her lack of interest in sex is his fault, not her physiology. She can leave him books or write notes describing how she would be interested in receiving love from him. I can guarantee that even if he does not like reading, he will read these notes or books.

A woman often needs to make plans in order to enjoy sex much more than her husband does. She needs to understand her own cycle and when she will be the most interested. Typically, before she can fully enjoy the experience, she needs to make sure there will be plenty of time to relax, taking measures for privacy, and allowing ample romantic lead-up time.

## He Needs You To Want To Release The Tension That Is Building In Him

A wife usually does not have the intimacy need that her husband has, but she can demonstrate that she loves him by making sure that his sexual needs (not wants or fantasies) are met. A man needs his wife to plan every few days to sexually engage. This should not be done with an "I-have-to-wash-the-dishes" attitude but should involve an attitude that communicates love and "I want your best." This type of attitude will go a long way to opening up the possibility of correction and redirection in other areas of your husband's life.

As mentioned before, a wife can, and should (from time-to-time), initiate sexual relations before his cycle reaches its peak. In this way, she demonstrates that she understands him and cares for him. Remember, one of the ways a man understands love is if his wife initiates meeting the need. In many men's minds, her lack of initiation or interest is seen as a rejection of him as a person. Initiating sexual contact is a way of demonstrating love for him in a man's language. A wife's willingness to meet this seemingly endless need speaks volumes to a man. It often establishes a bond that will keep him from straying.

## Marital Exercise #9

### Resolve to Meet His Intimacy Needs

Prepare in your heart to meet his intimacy needs consistently for the rest of his life. Ask God for His help in fulfilling this all-important role in your husband's life. It is at the center of His will for your marriage, so you can be assured He will help you in this way.

Draw your husband to you through his need for sexuality by initiating, inventing new ways to fulfill his need, and adding elements of surprise at times. Expand your own sexual vocabulary and understanding so that you may meet your husband's need in this area. A few suggestions would be to:

*Read books.*
*Talk to godly women who are satisfied in their marriage.*
*Read magazine articles addressing this issue.*
*Pray a prayer that says something like:*

> "Dear Lord, You have made us to be united in love together physically, emotionally, mentally, and spiritually. What an awesome gift you have given us to experience each other's bodies and find pleasure in them. For whatever reason, you have created us differently and with different needs. Help me, Lord, as his wife, to meet that loud and deep need within him. Give me empathy to his plight and struggle. Make me in-tune with his needs and then give me the energy, attitude, and desire to fill it. It's truly a gift you've given us. May I never forget that.
>
> In Jesus' Name,
> Amen."

## He Wants You To "Listen" To His Soul During Physical Intimacy

Many men cannot put into words the emotions and thoughts that they are feeling; they express these through the intimate encounters with their wife. It is the wise wife who realizes that her husband is trying to say something through how he has sex. He will open up to the woman who lovingly meets this need and who gently asks questions before, during, and after the sexual encounter. In many ways, physical intimacy is the way he shares his feelings and emotions of his life. We will spend considerable time on developing the ability to listen in the last chapter of this book.

If a wife really wants to know what her husband is dreaming, thinking, feeling, and worrying about, she must understand that it is within the context of expressing his sexuality that he will most likely tell her. In fact, it is in this experience that he is most likely to understand himself. There is a reason why most affairs are said to be hurried sex followed by good listening. A man wants a consistent lover who will listen to his soul during the physical intimacy.

## Marriage Exercise #10

### Signaling Intimacy

How do you or your husband signal interest in sexual relations? There are a number of ways to let your partner know you are interested in sex, but what I have found is that most couples have fallen into a rut or have an inadequate means of letting each other know that *now* would be a good time. Work through a few possible ways of letting your partner know you are interested. Here are a few ideas we came up with to help you:

**Direct request.** This is where either husband or wife just says directly, "I would like to have sex with you." Some couples use this method easily and with joy. Others find that stating their request directly and openly takes the romance and joy out of the encounter.

**Indirect request.** Many couples use the indirect method to signal interest in sexual relations. "I would like to spend some time with you later. What do you think?" A rolling of the eyes towards the bedroom can also be an indirect request or casual compliments like, "You look beautiful tonight!"

**Verbal signal.** Some couples (like those with young children) find it hard to find almost any times of privacy in which they could make their need or interest in sexual relations known. One couple I know invented a verbal symbol that the children would not understand to say that they were interested in having sexual relations. It could be a reference to pot roast or a particular vacation like the Grand Canyon.

**Tangible signal.** One couple found it awkward to always have to ask for sexual fulfillment, so they placed two normal looking figurines on the mantel—a man and a woman. They were normally facing forward. The partner interested in sex would turn their figurine toward the other figurine. This was a gentle way of saying "I am interested in being with you sexually" without having to actually request an encounter. It worked for this couple.

**Always interested.** Some wives can just assume that their husbands are interested in sex at all times, so the only variable is whether she is ready or has any interest or time. This is where a wife should understand her husband's sexual cycle and plan for a sexual encounter or release at those intervals as best she can. It may not be easy or convenient at all times, but it is necessary to try to meet the need somehow.

# Chapter 7

# Companionship

*Titus 2:3-5; Genesis 2:18*

Kelly had fallen in love with Steve. They had been dating for a year and a half, and she really hoped he wanted to get married so they could develop a life together. But Steve loved baseball. If he couldn't go personally, he watched every game that his beloved Dodgers played on television. He was seriously considering renting an apartment close to Dodger Stadium to make it easier to attend the games.

Their romantic relationship was up and down at times and never seemed to approach marriage. From Kelly's point of view, Steve was obsessed and she just couldn't understand it. He was literally building his life around his baseball team. From his point of view, it was a healthy pursuit of a sport he loved. She came to see me about the fact that Steve would just not commit to the relationship. They loved each other and talked about building a family, but he would not commit. What could she do to change this?

I was aware of her hope that Steve would get over his focus on baseball. I recommended that if she wanted to move Steve toward a committed relationship, she would need to enter into his world, going to as many baseball games as he was interested in taking her to. Rather than changing him or trying to get him to grow up, she would need to become his companion in his pursuit of baseball.

She began doing this, and the relationship was moving forward to the place where a number of us thought he was about to pop the question. But she abruptly broke up with him. "I can't do it!" she said. "I can't act as though this stupid game is important. I can't pretend that I enjoy it and that he doesn't need to grow up." She came to realize what it would take to be married to this man and decided she could not be his companion. This was actually a wise decision on her part because of her inflexibility with his passion for baseball. She could not get over the fact that it seemed infantile. "Surely he must see that this is a junior high pursuit!" she exclaimed at one point.

What she could not see was that Steve had locked on to baseball as his hobby and enjoyment. If anyone wanted to get close to him, they were going to have to like baseball. This was the door into his soul. If a woman he was dating did not enjoy or learn to enjoy baseball, then he could not get serious about her. She would never truly understand him because he tended to explain all things in his life through baseball analogies and stories of winning and losing. He was a good man who worked hard and wanted to marry and settle down, but he had a hobby he wasn't willing to give up because it allowed him to express himself and his feelings. Kelly did not feel that she could learn companionship with this sport, so she took a pass on Steve.

I have talked with countless wives who have the same attitude Kelly has about their husband's hobby. It could be car racing, cycling, photography, football, bird watching, music, a particular musical group, motorcycles, investing, stamp collecting, woodworking, reading, a civic cause, politics, missions, cooking, airplanes, or a hundred other different hobbies. Many women feel their husbands need to grow up and stop being so passionate about activities that seem to them a waste of time. There are more important things to spend time on after all. These women, often without realizing it, want their husbands to become like their girlfriends and enjoy the activities they enjoy or do the things they deem worthwhile and important. This just won't happen. Men like the recreational pursuits they like because it clicks emotionally, mentally, and spiritually with the man they are.

Men open their souls from a different door than a woman. Typically, it is through his hobby, passion, or work. If a wife does not understand these things, she can't understand him fully because he will not share who he really is with her. He will open the treasures of his soul only to those who understand his world, his competitions, his passions, and his codes.

## Scriptural Explanation

God highlights this need in men by how He instructs women in Titus 2:3-5.

> *Older women likewise are to be reverent in their behavior, not malicious gossips nor enslaved to much wine, teaching what is good, so that they may encourage the young women to love their husbands, to love their children, to be sensible, pure, workers at home, kind, being subject to their own husbands, so that the word of God will not be dishonored. (NASB)*

God knows that a man opens up to his companions. He trusts them. What is God's solution to this regular dilemma of married life? Learning companionship love. A man needs his wife to be his companion in some sense of that word. The word *love* in the above passage is the Greek word *phileo,* which is a brotherly love, a friendship love, and a companionship love—not a self-sacrificial love. It is interesting that women are never commanded to sacrificially love their husbands because they seem to do this naturally—it's inherent in their nature. But they *are* commanded to develop the ability to meet their husbands' need for a female companion.

Being his true companion is a sure way of filling up your husband. He wants to share his life with you. In fact, it is one of the main reasons why he agreed to marry you in the first place. During the dating phase, chances are you gave a number of indications that you were willing to be his companion in the activities, ideas, and lifestyle he found so fascinating. This word connotes *friendship,* so by commanding women to *phileo* love their husbands, God is saying that women need to make sure to learn how to become the friend of their husband. In other words, it is something that is learned and does not often come naturally. This is why the Apostle Paul instructs older women who have had successful marriages to show younger women how to do this unnatural thing.

I have talked with a number of women who really struggle with having his kind of fun or wanting to being absorbed in his business dealings. But in some form or another, he wants you to be his companion—to walk through life with him as his friend. You might try to think of this kind of love as a side-by-side love— enjoying a common interest and activity together. Most women are much more interested in communicating their feelings, thoughts, and ideas face-to-face. But most men are not wired that way. Instead, they express their feelings, thoughts, and ideas in a secondary context that is objectively distant from them. Side-by-side love communicates these things while participating in a common interest or activity at the same time.

Let me give you an example of this. After my grandmother passed away, my grandfather married a woman who was the definition of elegance and high society. I was amazed one day when I saw her in a fishing boat with my grandfather. She was dressed in one of the most elegant fishing outfits I have ever seen; but she was out there with her new husband, enjoying what he enjoyed. There are reasons why more marriages succeeded fifty years ago. One of those reasons is that women generally understood that a man wants a woman to be with him, doing things that he finds enjoyable.

## Risks of Need Not Met

Refusing to become your husband's companion is not an option if you want a great marriage. In fact, it is a requirement. The door to his soul may seem infantile, silly, or unappealing; but I assure you that it is usually the only way to the inner core of this man. It is not uncommon for women to fake interest in a man's activities during the dating and courtship phases in order to win him over. On one level she is interested in the activity because he is involved in it. But as is often the case, this willingness to be with him dwindles away after a few months or years of marriage, and it becomes work. In a way, this "I-was-interested-while-we-were-dating" is a form of false advertising. Many men select their spouse by her willingness to engage in the activities they both find fascinating. In the depth of their hearts, men are saying:

*"Finally, someone who will go the races with me."*

*"She really likes football."*

*"This is the first girl I have met who really understands my business."*

*"She seems fascinated by all the people and activities that make up my day."*

I believe there are three main risks a wife takes when she doesn't meet this need for companionship. The first risk is a major one, and should be scary enough to convince you to try as hard as you can. It makes sense that the woman who enjoys a man's recreational or passionate pursuits will be the one accepted into his soul. Why? Because we know this is the door to his soul where he shares himself fully. This is why most affairs for men start at work or through recreation. Any woman who saddles up next to him and is willing to listen to him talk about these areas that consume him is ushered into his soul as an honored guest. Someone who is willing to work or play side-by-side with him and talk in the terms that fill his world always sparks temptation for this could-be soul mate. How tragic that every man who gets married is looking for a soul mate, but many wives refuse to go through the only door to his soul.

A second risk comes when a wife allows herself to become selfish and focuses exclusively on the activities and hobbies she is most interested in. She may enjoy herself tremendously, but in the meantime a chasm opens up between her and her husband. It is not that a wife or husband needs to give up the things they enjoy most, but they must have plenty of activities with the other person that they enjoy doing together too. If you are only putting up with the activity for the sake of the marriage, then you won't really experience feelings of joy and the two of you will grow distant.

Lastly, the third risk relates to one of the great dangers of married life—routine, boredom, and drudgery. If a husband and wife don't have enjoyable activities and pursuits together, he begins to experience drudgery, boredom, and problems whenever he is with his wife and family. His focus can tend to shift toward sources of really enjoyable activities (other than physical intimacy) with his other friends or colleagues. This is not a recipe for attraction and commitment.

Ladies, your husband wants you to be his companion in something. It could be in business or recreation or charity; but whatever it is, figure out a way to be with him in his passionate pursuits. If you are not willing to work hard at learning how to love your husband as a friend, you may doom your marriage to a businesslike relationship in which two people share a home, children, and a few other things.

Many women attempt to get their husbands to join them in activities they are excited about. This may improve a marriage in the short term, but it does not open up his soul, which is the goal. This only works if he is passionate about an area. Companionship in less passionate areas are not as rewarding to him. Be his companion in something he is excited and passionate about, and you will experience a whole new man.

## How to Access His Soul

The door to a woman's soul generally opens through gentle and honest conversation. The doorway to a man's soul is first through companionship (the activity itself) accompanied by active-detached listening (which we will explain further in Chapter 9). A man unconsciously reasons that his wife is not interested in knowing him if she will not share his passions with him. He figures this must be true because this is one of the only doors in or out of his soul. To many women, this seems ridiculous. She thinks, "Why don't you just tell me what you are feeling or tell me what you are thinking?" as this is the way a woman would communicate. But a man – who has less connecting fibers between the left side and the right side of his brain and who is generally less in touch with his feelings and more linear in his thinking – is not capable of just telling you his feelings outright. He operates in the context of something he enjoys or is passionate about. He needs the analogies, words, codes, initials, and stories of that world to express them.

God never asks us to do the things that come naturally for us. This is why God commands men to give themselves sacrificially to their wives in Ephesians 5:25. That is why at first this command, "...to love their husbands," seems so out of place when directed toward wives. Wives don't usually need to be trained to give themselves sacrificially for their husbands—they do this much more naturally than men do. As mentioned earlier, this command for older women to train younger women to love their husbands is a different form of the word *love* than a sacrificial meeting of needs. The word *love* in this case is not *agape*, which is sacrificial love – the kind of love that God demonstrated through sending His Son Jesus Christ. Rather, the word for *love* is *phileo*—friendship love. This is the kind of love that companions share while enjoying the same thing together. It is shoulder-to-shoulder enjoying one another—playing together. The Apostle Paul says that wives need to be trained to really embrace the role of companion and friend. Men so desperately need and want this companion to be their wives, and they don't realize that it does not come naturally for them.

Let me show you how one wife's attempt to exercise companionship love with her husband took their marriage to a whole new level. Ross and Debbie had a functional marriage. But Debbie could not get Ross to talk about anything with her. In fact, he seemed non-communicative. He talked to his friends about how much he loved her, his thoughts, all about his business, and the people he worked with; but it was difficult to really talk with her. From her end, they had a good marriage but little connection. At one point when her husband's business was in a difficult period, he asked her to get involved in his business with him.

She took advantage of this opportunity and dove into his world, significantly helping the business. Better yet, their marriage went to another level. Everything he was thinking and feeling and wanted to talk with her about now had a set of common experiences she could relate to. In order for their marriage to go to the next level, she needed to become his companion at work so that she could really understand his struggles, joys, obstacles, and rewards. He needed her more than he ever realized. Their marriage and business improved dramatically. When she moved into this new companion role, everything changed. Their marriage not only survived, it thrived. Few women understand the importance their husbands place on them for being their companions.

## Marriage Exercise #1

## Exploring Companionship

What three activities (besides intimacy) is your husband thinking about all the time? It is in these three areas that he wants and needs you to be his companion. Often it is work, a hobby, and/or family; but it could be something else like home, money, and relatives. The circumstances of your life may preclude you from being as involved as both of you would like but think this through and plan for times when you can engage.

*Work*                          *Self*
*Hobby*                         *Church / Charity*

*Family (immediate/parents)*      *Community/Politics*
*Finances*                        *Friends*

## Understanding the Basics of Friendship and Companionship

One of the main reasons a man gets married is to have a life-long companion—someone to share his life with who gives evidence that she really enjoys his interests, pursuits, career, and ideas. He needs this or he will not usually commit to marrying her. In order to give wives an increased ability to meet this companionship need in their husbands, it is helpful to understand the basics of friendship. These six basic insights will allow you to become deeper friends with your husband as well as increase the friendships in your life.

1. **Friendship begins with sharing basic information.**

   To become close friends with someone, the basic elements of friendship must be built into the relationship. The first step in becoming a friend with another person is to exchange basic information in the various categories of life. These are not necessarily deep opinions or probing insights; these are just the frameworks for how you approach life. If a friendship is to move forward, there must be an understanding and agreement there. This means that two people must communicate information typically about the nine relationships of life: God, self, marriage, family, work, church, money, society, and friends. Some questions to consider:

   *What does the other person understand about each of these areas?*

   *What do they hope to see happen in each of these relationships?*

   *What do they know or not know about these relationships?*

*What types of relationships does the person have in these areas?*

This is the first step toward friendship. It begins with your name and basic personal information and grows through sharing information in each relationship. Friendship can hit a wall at any point if either side of the equation is no longer willing to share their basic information. If one person stops being willing to share, then the friendship stops growing or stops altogether.

What is your husband's basic information in each of these areas? Has it changed since you have known him? Is he at a point of change in any of these relationships in in his life? These are the types of things that friends know about one another.

2. **Friendship depends upon sharing things in common.**

Friendship can't deepen without a common activity or interest to share together. Many women ignore this step or want to skip over it and move right on to sharing the deep feelings, needs, and thoughts of close friends. But sharing a common activity or interest is an essential part of the process. For most men, this is the most enjoyable part of friendship. They absolutely love standing side-by-side with someone who enjoys doing the same thing they enjoy doing. It provides the essential context for deeper conversations later. For many men, the side-by-side sharing of a common interest is the definition of friendship and their need for companionship. They may not even see the talking and interacting that comes as a part of these activities.

Many women would like the shared interest to be the family; but for most men, the shared activity must be more than the family. He envisions his wife fishing with him, watching football with him, golfing, skiing, bird watching, listening to concerts—something he can focus his interests, talents, emotions, and desires toward. Each man wants to share his favorite activities with his chosen bride. The privilege of having a companion means having someone by his side during the really enjoyable things of his life. Remember that he sees this aspect of getting close to him as a process around the activity. Often face-to-face interchanges are too emotional and produce great tension in him.

Keep in mind that a large part of the focus is on the activity, not each other. That is why he may ask, "Do you like _____?" or "Are you having a good time?" or "You really don't like this, do you?" He wants you to enjoy the thing itself or else he feels you can never understand why he enjoys it so much or what he feels when he enjoys it.

A man reveals some aspects of who he is in the things he likes doing. He explains himself in a way when he really gets into certain things. It may explain what happened in his past, his latent talents, interest, or desires. It may even display the dominant influences in his life or his internal struggles.

3. **Friendship deepens when there is a common perspective within that common activity or interest.**

The next important step in the building of a solid friendship is to discover what common perspectives you share. Friendship means some common point of view is communicated and shared between two friends. Differing viewpoints are usually marginalized or else they will begin to destroy the friendship. Review the nine relationships of life with your husband and think through the various perspectives in each relationship. Do you know what his perspective is on various issues? Is your husband at a changing point in his life about any of these areas or issues?

4. **Friendship expands when a common struggle is shared.**

A friendship needs a common struggle or a common cause in order to move to the next level. A shared common cause begins to build a new level of depth and interconnection to each other. There are all kinds of crises or needs that may provide this bonding: financial, emotional, military, sports, relational, national, and so on. The process of meeting that need together bonds two people.

There are times when the shared need is the need of only one party. This is where one of the friends agrees to hold the need of the other as a significant focus for their own life. This "your need is my need" mentality also builds a powerful bonding. In many cases, this kind of sacrificial holding of another's need as your own creates a strong marriage. If a husband or a wife refuses to embrace the needs of the other person, the marriage will become a business relationship at best, and an emotional isolation ward with eventual separation or divorce at worst.

A wife or husband can decide to move toward close friendship with their spouse just by committing to doing the first four steps and, most importantly, holding the need of the other person as their own. Letting go of selfishness to support and build up the other person is how deep and lasting marriages are formed.

5. **Friendship matures with common memories.**

A friendship develops its own history. True friends start talking about things they have done together. This recounting of its own history is a sign of a deepening friendship. Common memories through pictures, letters, mementos, gifts, and so on, move the friendship further down the road. Many times, a husband will need to be reminded of all the great memories the couple or family has shared. This can be done through pictures, storytelling, and the like. If this is not done regularly, they will only live in the present, which may be either good or bad at that moment. I know of marriages that have been significantly repaired by getting a husband and wife to recount old stories of happier times together.

A couple of ideas to try are to:

*Display pictures around the house of your good times together.*

*Talk about great memories that you have had together.*

*Keep mementos of good times all around the house or office.*

6. **Friendship is cemented when feelings are expressed and shared.**

Feelings must be shared and received in order to have an intimate friendship. The sharing and receiving of common feelings opens the crucial doorway to intimacy. When a friend shares their feelings, they need to be listened to. It is not the time to correct misperceptions, mistakes, or poor judgments. If they want correction, they will ask for it. If the feeling is acknowledged and understood, the friendship is helped and sustained; but if the feeling is ignored, the friendship suffers or ceases. If both parties actually feel the same emotion at the same time, the opportunity for deep connection is greatly increased.

When a man is willing to talk about his feelings, he wants his wife to share that feeling with him by focusing on what he is feeling. In other words, she should not think about what she is feeling at that moment, how she will react to his feelings or actions, what the solution will be, or what he will most likely do. (This describes active-detached listening.) Remember, husbands are not as comfortable swimming in the emotional pond as most women. Emotions are unpredictable and often destructive in his world. He may need a lot of encouragement and support as he shares his feelings.

When a man says to his wife or girlfriend, "I need you with me," or "I would like you to be with me," he is expressing this companionship need. Her support, listening ear, observation, leadership, presence, and involvement are invaluable to him.

### Marriage Exercise #2

### Companionship Planning

If he has a need that you do not share, it will not go away through avoidance. Men will either stuff the need – which may explode later (often during mid-life) – or he will connect with other people who will meet this need. Either way, it is something to take seriously. Think about the following questions and plan out how you will become an ideal companion for your husband.

*What are the activities, hobbies, and interests your husband had before you were married?*

*Would you be willing to spend two to four hours per week or month in order to fulfill your husband and have a great marriage?*

*Are there activities you would be willing to try that he might be interested in?*

*Are there new ways to enjoy being a part of his hobbies, activities, interests, and so on?*

185

## Becoming His Companion

If spending two to six hours a week focused on something could significantly improve your marriage, would you do it? If so, it takes some work and involves finding some activities you two can enjoy together. It is understandable to have your own interests and hobbies and those are important too. But focus should be spent on the activities and interests you share together. Those will be the things that become central in keeping the relationship intact, especially once the kids are gone.

Whatever your husband is into is what he is into. As long as it is not immoral, illegal, or illicit, it is OK. For some reason it connects with who he is, and the people in it are his kind of people. Embracing his "thing" will go a long way toward deepening your marriage. Joy in marriage comes through depth of relationship, and you must understand what the other person is like in order to go deep.

Let me demonstrate my point. Joanne was a wonderful wife. She and her husband had all boys. Her husband and their sons were into motorcycles and dirt. Her husband, Gary, discovered motorcycle racing as a way to stay close to the boys. He and the boys were really into it—practicing every day after school, racing on the weekends, repairing the bikes through long nights in the garage. At first, Joanne did not want anything to do with the motorcycles—they were too dangerous for her. She was especially scared when they went to the races. She begged off going a few times until Gary sat down with her and told her, "Honey, I know that you don't like this and it is hard on you, but the boys love this and I love being with them. We don't need you to do much—just be in the stands, watch our races, and wave occasionally. That would be great."

186

So every Friday night Joanne brought her blanket, hot coffee, a good book, and a thick foam pad for the bleachers. She became the companion to her husband and her boys that they needed. It made all the difference in his heart and kept him deeply connected to her. She didn't understand how it worked, but it was obvious that it did.

It is not uncommon for a woman to be open to experiencing a particular activity if it is at a higher level or in a more refined way. Most wives who have participated with their husband in his activity observed another couple taking part in the same activity in a way that would be more enjoyable from her point of view. Once she sees she can do it another way, she's all in.

If a wife wants to minister to her husband's deepest needs, then she will think through various ways to be more of his companion in activities that he finds deeply thrilling and engaging. If it has been awhile, she may need to initiate engagement in his activities on her own because he may have given up hope that she would ever want to do these things. He may be willing to go and have a good time if the details of the outing and activity are arranged. Remember, this issue is all about being his companion (his friend), not a romantic time for the wife. It may be hard not to think of it this way, but we want to head off any resentment if things don't go the way she thinks they should romantically.

Years ago, I left the pastorate of a church in southern California to become a pastor to pastors in a region of northern California. One of the most difficult things about this new job was that my wife no longer participated in my ministry. Not having her understanding, input, interaction, and insights was a tremendous loss. I missed being able to have her hear my sermons and talk about them. I missed discussing people that she knew and the problems she understood. We worked to make up for the loss of work companionship in every possible way.

## Marriage Exercise #4

## Becoming His Companion

Circle the activities that you both enjoy or would be willing to try.

| | | | |
|---|---|---|---|
| Building Things | Watching Baseball | Darts | Cooking |
| Crafts | Hiking | Frisbee golf | Writing |
| Racing | Working out | Archery | Acting |
| Working on cars | Karate | Flying ultra-light planes | Community Projects |
| Sewing | Judo | Sailing | Disabled |
| Crochet | Improvisational games | Motor boating | Ministries |
| Cricket | Learning | Nature walks | Special seeds |
| Volleyball | Flying | Flying RC | Books on tape |
| Football | Bike riding | Airplanes | Driving |
| Basketball | Jogging | Beach | Painting |
| Spear fishing | Amusement parks | Beach games | Auto |
| Swimming | Roller coasters | Horseback riding | Repair/detailing |
| Snow skiing | Pets | Going out to eat | White water rafting |
| Cross country skiing | Pin ball | Fishing | Picnic games |
| Tubing, | Air hockey | Aerobics | Laser tag |
| Tobogganing | Table games | Pottery | Rock climbing |
| Snowmobiling | Playing/making Music | Antiquing | Canoeing |
| Motorcycles | Singing | Boat shows | Kayaking |
| ATV | Parties | Home & garden shows | Historic sites |
| 4 Wheeling | Baking | RV Shows | Conventions |
| Reading | Drawing | Bowling | Retreats |
| Watching T.V. | Modeling | Bike riding | Speaking |
| Movies | Snorkeling | Hang gliding | Backpacking |
| Eating | Scuba | Sky diving | Triathlon |
| Sleeping | Rollerblades | Museum | Marathons |
| Tennis | | | Soccer |
| | | | Quilting |

| Racquetball | Roller hockey | Prof sports | Embroidery |
|---|---|---|---|
| Golf | Ice hockey | tickets | Bow hunting |
| Talking | Ice skating | Spelunking | Rifle hunting |
| Water-skiing | Camping | Mountain | Investing |
| Boating | Competitive | Climbing | Calligraphy |
| Traveling | running | Gardening | Video games |
| Photography | Softball | Woodworking | Arcades |
| Developing | Water parks | Bird watching | Shuffleboard |
| pictures | Horseshoes | Shopping | Table tennis |
| Cooking | Beach volleyball | Used book | Wind surfing |

## Marriage Exercise #5

### Sharing His Top Three Worlds

The top three worlds that men want to share with their wives are typically work, hobbies, and friends.

1. What part of these worlds would your husband like to share with you?

2. What practical ways can you engage as a more intriguing companion to your husband each week?

   *Speaking and Listening:*

   *Actions and Involvement:*

   *Attitude:*

   *Writing:*

# Four Types of Companionship

A man wants a woman who will be his companion in one of four different ways: a watcher, a cheerleader, a participant, or a coach. Different men want or need their wives to emphasize these roles in different ways. As a wife it is helpful to evaluate when and in what areas your husband is the most pleased with your involvement in his life:

*Is it when you watch or listen to him and are present at his performances?*

*Is it when you are his biggest fan and strongest supporter, acting as a cheerleader for him?*

*Is it when you are involved in the activity as much as he is, engaged and committed to a high degree?*

*Is it when you are directing, encouraging, coaching, or even leading him and others to their maximum potential?*

Most men will have a companionship role they would like their wives to play. It is possible that the role may change from work to recreation or from home to social settings. Realize that this need for companionship in most men ranks a close second to physical intimacy in importance. It is the radical wife who understands his need for companionship and seeks to love him by meeting that need in the best way that she can.

**The Watcher/Listener.** This is where the husband prefers to have his wife watch or listen to him pursue the work, activity, sport, or interest that excites him. He does not need or prefer her to participate in the event. If she is not physically present, then he may want her to listen to a blow-by-blow description of his exploits. He wants her to watch his performance, take notes, and observe carefully with focused attention. Most guys will want a play-by-play description of your positive reactions to his activities and interests. *Did you see that? Did you see when I did that?* Her presence validates his importance. This kind of man will often pick activities where spectators are common.

**The Cheerleader.** It may seem strange to say, but there are men who need fans. These men want and need to live in an environment of praise. They tend to gravitate to women who have an exalted opinion of them. This man really wants his wife to call out his good points to others, as sort of a form of bragging. Cheerleading can range from loud and organized cheering to quiet comments about how wonderful his actions, qualities, talent, and abilities are. You will notice that this kind of person actually does not feel like they are whole or complete without people noticing what they are doing. The cheerleader's role is almost like being the public relations person for him. He knows he can't brag about himself without looking prideful but you, his wife, can talk about him all the time. This is noble for you and wonderful for him. Some men use this as the major way to enhance their reputation.

**The Participant.** This is the type of husband who really wants his wife to participate with him in his activities. He has a great desire to have her involved with him in his activity or interest. He wants her to know the people and projects that he is working on, to do his hobby with him, and take lessons to get better so that they can discuss the nuances of the hobby. In that way he will be able to express his feelings through the metaphors of the hobby. He wants her to be side-by-side with him. Note: This role has been emphasized in Western culture in the last fifty years. The culture is placing more and more demands on wives to be full participants in their husband's activities; however, this participant role is not a role that every man needs or wants. It is also not a role that every wife can fulfill in the way that our culture describes it. Be careful that the cultural ideal of a great marriage does not become yours.

**The Coach.** This is where the husband really wants his wife to help, direct, encourage, and even lead him to maximum effectiveness and success. Many men really count on their wives to be this source of strength and motivation to succeed at a level that they never could without her. When this type of husband asks, "What do you think?" he is really asking for direction. He really wants to know what you think he should do. Many husbands want to use their wives in this mentoring, coaching, or secret-confidant role where she listens to his thoughts, strategies, and plans but then interacts with them. This type of approval from her is important and reassuring to him.

## Marriage Exercise #3

## Companionship Types

1. What type of companion does my husband generally desire me to be?

   Watcher/listener    Cheerleader    Participant    Coach

2. What type of companion am I naturally?

   Watcher/listener    Cheerleader    Participant    Coach

3. Which companionship role does my husband want me to have towards his work?

4. What companionship role does my husband want me to have towards his hobbies?

5. What companionship role does my husband want me to have towards our finances?

6. What companionship role does my husband want me to have towards church?

7. What companionship role does my husband want me to have in community involvement?

8. What companionship role does my husband want me to have toward his friends?

9. What companionship role does my husband want me to have toward his internal life?

10. What is my husband's dominant/favorite recreation?

11. How does he want me to participate in that?

## Resist Activities Where Sin, Perversion, Fear, or Anxiety Abound

A woman cannot and should not give into a man's desires to have his wife become a companion with him in anything sinful, perverse, or wicked. Also, she should not be forced into activities that create high levels of fear, worry, or anxiety in her or about her children. Some concerns will be normal about every type of activity but trying to participate in something that exposes your greatest fear should not be considered a part of becoming a godly wife.

Many men can be insensitive in this area because they do not have any concerns or problems with a particular activity. They cannot imagine that their wife would not trust them or push through their fear to join them in this activity. It is usually best to discuss your inability to participate in this activity with your husband, as opposed to ignoring the issue. It works best to have a conversation before the activity takes place. You could say something like: "Honey, I am becoming increasingly uncomfortable and troubled by my involvement in _____. I am sure that you enjoy doing that, but I am just not able to participate anymore. I know that you may not understand my inability, but I just can't. I hope you will respect my convictions (or feelings) in this area."

At this point, it might be helpful to suggest another activity or idea that would not violate your conviction or expose your fears. A wife, who has demonstrated love, caring, compassion, and a desire to be with her husband, will almost always be listened to in these types of interactions. Husbands generally want the best for their wives and wouldn't inflict harm on them intentionally. But, if needed, it is important that she be firm and consistent in her refusal to move in those directions. Note that her refusal does not necessarily mean she should limit his involvement in the activity; otherwise, he may grow resentful.

## Marriage Exercise #6

### Avoidance of Sin, Perversion, or Fear

*Does your husband want you to join him in activities that violate your conscience?*

*Does your husband want you to join him in activities that make you afraid, anxious, or worried?*

*How have you tried to decline or redirect your involvement?*

## A Truth To Remember

In order for something to be different in your marriage, something must change away from what you are presently doing. Many people want their marriage to improve, but they do not want to change personally to make it happen. If you are going to move your marriage in a positive direction, you may need to be the one willing to take some positive actions that minister to the deepest needs of your spouse. That means you will need to take a close look at yourself, eliminating any selfishness you may be guilty of (if any). Selfishness must go down and meeting the needs of your spouse must go up. These are the two secrets of successful marriage counseling.

## Marriage Exercise #7

## Growing Spiritually Deeper Together

Celebrate your faith in God together. It is a wonderful way to spend time together and will deepen your relationship in profound ways. Here are some ways you and your husband can grow deeper spiritually together.

*Pray together each day and night*

*Memorize Scripture together*

*Share quiet time and devotional material*

*Take a Bible study together*

*Join a small group from your church*

*Serve the Lord together*

# Chapter 8

## Attractive Soul & Body

*1 Timothy 2:9, 10; 1 Peter 3:3-5; Song of Solomon 1:15*

Rachel was a captivating woman. Even though most who knew her would not consider her physically attractive, you couldn't be around her without being completely enthralled. She took care of her physical appearance by working out, using makeup, and wearing attractive, stylish clothing; but she captivated her husband in a totally different way. He was completely drawn to her and deeply in love.

When they were dating, she competed for his attention with some really gorgeous women. At first no one thought they would keep dating because he was handsome and had a great career ahead of him. But he could not escape the fact that there was something different about her. After dating for some time, a wise counselor took him aside and pointed out that she was the best thing in his life, and he needed to marry this priceless treasure. At times he was amazed to find himself married to her. He was lucky to have her and he knew it. The longer they were married, the more attractive she became to him.

Rachel is the complete embodiment of the truths of this chapter. She did the best she could on her outward beauty, but she focused on the greatest beauty secret—her soul. She always had a quick smile and a warm greeting. She made you feel like you were special and important. She was almost manic in her ability to listen and express interest in others' ideas, topics, and opinions. She found reasons to be grateful and ways to be flexible. She was always positive. She served a great God who would work things out. Because her personality was so captivating, many men found her attractive. But most importantly, her husband found her attractive and loved her very much. Her husband's career placed him around beautiful women all the time, but Rachel's soul outshone the skin-deep beauty of other women.

What is the key component of an attractive soul? We tend to call it "attitude" – an aspect of a person we could view as "software" rather than "hardware." We have all seen women who are outwardly beautiful, but inwardly they are cold, calculating, ungrateful, bitter, demanding, and contentious. No one is drawn to this kind of a woman for very long. While the outward forms of beauty are important, it is the beautiful soul that is the most attractive long term.

We have all seen the successful rich man who marries the younger beautiful, trophy wife. Inevitably, a few years later he tires of her and marries another young, beautiful wife who looks a lot like the woman he just divorced. The beauty of externals fades if the attitude of the heart is not beautiful. It is a shame that there are no classes on how to develop a beautiful soul because this is the beauty secret that lasts.

Yes, it is important to be as outwardly beautiful and attractive as you can be for your husband, but it is not here that you will continue to attract him over time. Rather, it is the beauty of your soul. How do you know if your soul is beautiful or not? It's all about attitude. Ask yourself these questions:

*Does he enjoy being with you?*

*Does spending time with you cause him to forget his problems or is he reminded of them?*

*Does he find that when he is with you the world takes on a positive glow or a more pessimistic slant?*

*Do you feel the need to correct him constantly?*

*Do you complain about what he isn't doing or hasn't done?*

*Can he count on you to nag and demand?*

*Do you feel entitled to drain the bank account?*

*Does the whole world treat you badly?*

*Is bitterness written on your face?*

*Has someone hurt you and everybody can see it?*

These questions hit on the kind of attitude that causes a woman to become ugly and repulsive to her husband, one that is negative and demanding. But a truly beautiful woman forgives easily, digs for the positive, and allows God to deal with the rough edges of her husband.

Isabel was in her 70s when I met her. She shuffled when she walked and could barely see, yet she was the complete delight of her husband, Frank. He told me that she was the most beautiful woman in the world. He occasionally asked me to look at her as he described this gorgeous woman. "Isn't she beautiful?" he would ask. I would nod and be encouraged by the bond between this old man and his wife of more than 50 years. They had grown old and more beautiful together.

The flower of physical attractiveness had long ago faded, but she was a beautiful woman. Love, grace, joy, encouragement, and fun radiated out from her. Everyone liked her and Frank was still captivated by her after all this time. Isabelle had taken the time and effort to develop a beautiful soul, and through her soul she attracted and completely captured the heart of her husband. He still saw her as physically attractive because she was the person who was the most kind, generous, grateful, flexible, and encouraging to him. It is amazing how beauty is in the eye of the beholder.

## The Biblical Mandate: Inner and Outer Beauty

First Peter 3:3, 4 says, "Do not let your adorning be external—the braiding of hair and the putting on of gold jewelry, or the clothing you wear—but let your adorning be the hidden person of the heart with the imperishable beauty of a gentle and quiet spirit, which in God's sight is very precious." The Apostle Peter is not forbidding women from putting on dresses or wearing jewelry or fixing up their hair. But he is saying that when women want to make themselves beautiful, they should not be overly focused on external beauty. When a woman wants to be beautiful, she should develop a beautiful soul because this kind of beauty is much more lasting and profitable than just an attractive exterior. The NASB version of the verse above has the emphasis right when the word *merely* is added (v. 3). It is not that women shouldn't try to be attractive to their husbands; they should. The most significant addition for long-term attractiveness comes from a beautiful soul.

*The Living Bible* catches the idea in modern terms: "Don't be (overly) concerned about the outward beauty that depends on jewelry, or beautiful clothes, or hair arrangement. Be beautiful inside, in your hearts, with the lasting charm of a gentle and quiet spirit that is so precious to God."

## Cultivating Beauty Requires Discipline

A woman must have had some level of attractiveness to her husband when they met and married or he would not have committed to the relationship. It should come as no surprise that cultivating both external beauty and internal beauty requires discipline. The word, *cultivate,* means, "to foster the growth of, to nurture, refine, develop, or improve." In other words, we should all spend the time, energy, effort, and resources to cultivate and maintain what has been naturally given to us to be more pleasing to those around us. It requires effort, as it doesn't happen naturally on its own.

It takes discipline to remain attractive, and it takes even more discipline to become attractive with inner beauty. In 1 Peter 3:4, 5, the Apostle Peter is arguing against a woman focusing exclusively or excessively on her external beauty as a way of fulfilling her wifely duties or attracting her husband. He proclaims that there is a kind of beauty that is much more attractive and long lasting— inner beauty. God does not want you to neglect either one of these things, but more focus and attention should be spent on developing and maintaining inner beauty. It is the one that lasts and makes the highest impact in your husband's life.

Now it does seem that some women let themselves go physically after they get married, and they are no longer as physically attractive as they were in the dating phase. When that takes place, it may be that their souls have become rotten or ugly long before their external attractiveness was lost. Maybe they gave into the impulses of selfishness, laziness, pride, envy, and the like,

201

which led to the fading of their outward beauty. This lack of discipline can also be a symptom of something internal – possibly depression or a wound that needs to be addressed and healed so that her inner and outer beauty can be restored to a healthy level. It might require medical attention, counseling, or talking with a trusted friend or pastor.

## Marriage Exercise #1

### Becoming Inwardly Beautiful

First Peter 3:4,5 says, "Cultivate inner beauty, the gentle, gracious kind that God delights in. The holy women of old were beautiful before God that way, and were good, loyal wives to their husbands" *(TM)*. These questions address issues of what is needed to be inwardly beautiful. Some of them require hard, introspective, and honest work. Reflect on each one; perhaps journal your answers as you work through them. This will be time well spent.

1. A beautiful woman does her work without needing to be noticed or to be in charge. She throws herself into what needs to be done instead of keeping track of who notices that she is working. Does this describe you?

2. A beautiful woman has processed the pain in her life so it educates her but does not embitter her. She realizes that she will not be whole until she has talked through the tragedies of her life with a trusted friend or counselor. How could you do more of this?

3. A beautiful woman is flexible with the things she cannot change and does not hold on to unrealistic expectations for long. She realizes that anger and irritation are signals that her expectations are unrealistic for that moment. They may be the

way things should be but not the way things can be right now. She evaluates her expectations, changes them quickly to realistic ones, and aims towards those. What practical steps could you take to become more beautiful in this regard?

4. A beautiful woman deeply desires things to be done right, not just her way or to her advantage. She knows right and wrong and will predictably do things that are good and admirable instead of pursuing her own selfish wants. How could you do more of this?

5. A beautiful woman has forgiven the people who have wounded her and stands ready to forgive the new hurts that will come. How could you do more of this?

6. A beautiful woman injects purity, hope, and decency wherever she goes, lifting people up to think about noble, courageous, sacrificial, and giving actions. How could you do more of this?

7. A beautiful woman thinks about pure things and does not let her mind wander in the gutter of perversion, or think about getting back at those who hurt or wronged her. How could you do more of this?

8. A beautiful woman invests in bringing harmony to her surroundings. She has that wonderful ability to bring people together, to allow people to see their common purposes rather than what divides them. How could you do more of this?

9. A beautiful woman stands for what is right and will not compromise when it comes to right and wrong or the truth of her faith. How could you do more of this?

10. A beautiful woman uses her words to encourage and emotionally build up the people in her life. She learns to hold

her tongue if what she has to say is destructive and toxic. Does this describe you?

## Developing a Beautiful Soul

It is hard to describe something that is invisible but beautiful. The beautiful soul is completely invisible to the naked eye, but we know it when we see it and marvel at its effect. I can picture a number of women who had cynical, demanding, self-focused souls, who later changed to become radiant souls that drew their husbands, their children and friends. I remember Loren, who was all about herself and her children, but began to include in her thinking how to help her husband win. When she did this, he began to win in new ways at work, at home, at church. His confidence began to soar and Loren became attracted to her husband again. It all began with her development of a beautiful soul instead of the staying bitter and negative.

I can remember a beautiful celebrity who had maneuvered herself to become the next wife of an even bigger celebrity. She was interviewed and toasted for her looks, her love, and her dreams coming true. Yet she allowed the beauty of her soul to be damaged by the reality of the man she married. The cynicism and self-focus of her husband became her normal orientation and in a few years the marriage fell apart and the ugliness of the divorce began.

I just enjoyed watching the culmination of a complete marriage turn around. I baptized a man who had earlier threatened to divorce his wife because he was no longer interested in her. She is by all accounts a short, rotund woman on the outside; but she became a beautiful soul which captured her husband's heart and led him back to God. It saved their marriage. I celebrated with the whole family as the husband and their daughter were baptized. There was absolute delight on the face of this beautiful woman—it was priceless. Her marriage and family had made it; her beautiful soul was the glue that held the family together. I know it had to be hard and a great deal of work to stop rehearsing his flaws, to dig for the triple-win scenario, to stay flexible when she would rather be self-focused, and lower her expectations of what he should be doing. But she did it! Let her works cause those to praise her in the gates.

Like this woman, the beauty of your soul can shine through your physical body. It is far more important to work on your soul than to start another diet or purchase the right clothes. It may not be your normal personality to be positive, flexible, or others-oriented but start today to grow in these soul issues.

## Marriage Exercise #2

### Developing a Beautiful Soul

1. A beautiful soul is not selfish: It is a win-win-win soul. This is the person who looks for the choice that allows God to win, the other person to win, and you to win. It may take a little thought or planning, but there is a win-win-win solution to all problems.

    *Are there some things you are doing that really only amount to a win for you and a loss for your husband?*

    *Are there some actions or words you can add to your life that will produce wins for you, wins for your husband, and wins for God?*

2. A beautiful soul is flexible: It says, "How can we make this work?"

*Are there some areas where you have been hostile, rigid, and inflexible?*

*What are ways to make these areas work without hostility?*

3. A beautiful soul is realistic with its expectations.

*In what areas do you have unrealistic expectations?*

*What are more reasonable expectations in the above areas?*

## Risks of Refusing to Develop a Beautiful Soul

What happens when a woman refuses to develop a beautiful soul? Unfortunately, the risks can be high. A wife, who does not stay grateful or allows her expectations to rise so high that her husband cannot meet them without a Herculean effort, may start to see less and less of him. He finds reasons not to be home. Everyone, including your husband, needs to be accepted, admired, and appreciated. A difficult, demanding, and bitter wife drains the energy right out of him; and so he begins to invent ways to be away from her. Some women determine that being demanding and unsatisfied will actually motivate their husbands to get things done. The problem is that this attitude destroys the relationship— even in the midst of the tasks being accomplished! It may feel like you won the battle, but really you're losing the war.

Why is a fiancé so beautiful to her bridegroom? It is because she is trying to please her future husband. She magnifies his strengths and abilities. She is naïve to some of his faults. She overlooks his weaknesses or recasts them as strengths or being fixable. It is this open soul that is especially attractive to men. If a woman loses this beauty, it is the beginning of the end of a beautiful relationship.

206

Ladies, it is true that your husband is not perfect. It is true that he has major weaknesses. It is true that he does not have a clue about some of the things that matter deeply to you. But this is also true of every man and woman on the planet. Every one of us is deeply flawed. When people get married, they enter into an agreement to stay open to each other unless the legality or immorality of their actions prevents openness. Work hard to maintain the kind of soul that is open to him—the kind that is encouraging, peaceful, and calm.

## Do You Attract or Repel?

The word *attractive* means, "to pull to or draw toward oneself or itself." Physical attractiveness may be something that initially draws your husband to you, but an attractive soul is what keeps him close by. The following qualities and actions comprise an attractive soul: gratitude, tranquility, respectful, flexible, and delightful. When we meet a person with a beautiful soul, we find ourselves encouraged and uplifted. We naturally want to be around them more. A husband is drawn to a wife with these qualities.

Unfortunately, some women are repellant—they discourage and drive people away. Many women have no idea how they have allowed their souls to rot. They don't realize they are not that enjoyable to be around. An ugly soul is gloomy, selfish, demanding, proud, pessimistic, contentious, prickly, negative, argumentative, bitter, and full of high expectations. It doesn't matter what this kind of person looks like—they are repellant. God wants to set the record straight about what a man needs from his wife. He needs her to continue to develop an attractive soul so that he finds himself drawn to this woman and captivated by her long term (Proverbs 21:9,19).

207

## Marriage Exercise #4

## Becoming Attractive to Him

Some women think that what they have right now is good enough. They say things like, "I don't want to change. I want him to change so my needs will be met." Spend some time asking yourself these questions. Take an honest assessment. It is not enough to just read these words or think about these areas, you must identify the areas that require development or smoothing out. If change is needed, then you must make an effort to change. It will be hard at times and requires discipline, but it can be done with God's help. This is part of the price of having a good marriage. Are you willing to pay that price?

1.  What can I as a wife do to develop an attractive soul and body?

2.  In what areas am I tempted to let myself go and no longer work on inner and outer beauty?

3.  What practical ways can I develop my soul to become more beautiful? (Evaluate each area. Decide if you could improve.)

| | |
|---|---|
| *Prayer* | *Exercise* |
| *Sleep* | *Eating habits* |
| *Commitments* | *Meditation* |
| *Priorities* | *Bible study* |
| *Laughter* | *Friendships* |
| *Smiling* | *Attitude* |
| *Touching* | *Tone of voice* |

## Qualities of Inner Beauty

God directs women to develop two key qualities of inner beauty: a *gentle and quiet spirit* (1 Peter 3:4). The beauty of our soul moves more and more to the forefront as our bodies continue to age. We need to spend some time understanding these two qualities because they form the basis of a beautiful or attractive soul.

### Gentleness

The word translated *gentle* in 1 Peter 3:4 is the Greek word *praus* which means, "gentle, meek, mild, flexible." Most commentators tell us that it is extremely difficult to translate this Greek word by one English word because in the English *meek, mild, and gentle* usually conveys a position of weakness or an overall lack of strength and character. However, the Greek word does not have any weakness in it at all. The idea is really closer to "voluntary flexibility." It is a readiness to adapt and adjust one's expectations to God's will and to others' needs according to the circumstances.

A large part of developing this positive quality of gentleness is how you handle expectations. A hope can become an expectation quickly. A rigid or excessively high expectation is what always leads to anger or some expression of selfishness. One insightful man said that anger is the result of unreasonable or unmet expectations. Unreasonable expectations and an unwillingness to adjust quickly are like huge warts on our soul. This inflexibility repels people. We all have a tendency to turn our desires into expectations without considering others' desires or goals. While this may be how we move forward toward our goals, it increases the likelihood that we will get angry or moody.

A woman with a beautiful soul will have the positive quality of being flexible or adaptable, especially to expectations. Anyone who is always ready to adapt and stay flexible to changing situations, desires, and needs is more welcome than the rigid person, who must have it their way and grows angry, moody, sullen, or depressed if things don't go according to their plan. A wife with flexible qualities becomes such a welcome part of her husband's life that he can't imagine life without her. He is drawn to her and her willingness to try new things, adjusting on the fly to the realities of life.

Practically, this might look like a willingness to lower her expectations about what her husband will (should) do, how the perfect vacation will go, or what "perfect" children are like. Now being gentle does not mean that she is flexible about her moral order. A godly wife does not adapt to that which is morally wrong. She does not lower her conscience to fit into her husband's world, but she is willing to adjust quickly in non-essential areas to keep the relationship enjoyable and moving along. The positive, attractive quality of flexibility means that she is always ready to adjust her expectations and reconfigure plans to incorporate new realities.

Sometimes it is easier to understand this concept when we see it in the opposite form. When a woman is always on the rampage because things did not go her way, she is the opposite of gentle or meek. When a wife is harping and nagging and demanding, she not only has a poor way of expressing her expectations; but she also repels those around her. All of us have seen the inflexible, demanding person who must have things their way or they melt down or threaten to melt you down. We avoid these people at every opportunity. This avoidance factor works in marriage also. If your husband finds that you are demanding, inflexible, moody, angry, or withering in your criticism of him, he will find ways to avoid you. Biblical meekness is positive flexibility that has a gentle, non-demanding quality to it—it is not weak and limp. It is gentle.

In the Old Testament, Abigail, the wife of Nabal, is a prime example of this powerful, positive quality of flexibility (1 Samuel 25). When she understood what her husband had done and what David would most likely do, she swung into action with a completely different plan to protect and save her husband and family. Her willingness to adjust and give large quantities of food and beverage to David showed her leadership and also her positive flexibility. Her diplomacy with David kept him from acting out the anger and murder that he was planning—she was brilliant! David praised her for averting tragedy, and he was also completely captivated by her soul. So much so, that after her husband died a few weeks later, he asked Abigail to marry him. It was the beauty of her soul that attracted David and likely saved this widow's life.

## Marriage Exercise #5

## Attractive Soul: Gentleness

### *Flexibility and Dealing with Expectations*

Life is a constant battle with varying expectations. Which ones are reasonable and which ones need to be adjusted? What expectations should I have in this situation? What expectations need to be abandoned as unrealistic, and which ones should be pursued with dogged persistence? We must develop the ability to adjust and flex our expectations quickly with a minimum amount of pouting, demanding, anger, and whining. It can be hard to do sometimes, but it is necessary to develop a beautiful soul that is attractive to people and a joy to be around. The questions below will help you take an honest assessment in this area of flexibility and expectations.

1. How would your husband want you to be more flexible so as to fit more easily in his world?

2. In what areas are your expectations and his expectations at war?

3. What are your expectations for your husband, family, and life?

4. How rigid are your expectations for your husband and family?

5. Do you find yourself getting angry often? (This often suggests someone who regularly has unrealistic or inflexible expectations.)

   What or who do you get angry at the most? What unmet expectation is behind this anger?

   *Husband*

   *Family*

   *Personal life*

6. What are you doing to communicate those expectations?

7. How flexible are you in attaining those expectations?

8. Would your husband, family, and others agree with your expectations for them?

## Quiet Spirit

The second part of the apostle's description of a beautiful soul is the two words translated as "quiet spirit" (1 Peter 3:4), which are the Greek words *hesuchios pneuma*. The word *quiet,* or *hesuchios,* means "tranquil, peaceable, non-reactive, creating harmony."[1] The

212

idea clearly expresses that a wife has a beautiful, attractive soul when her husband can count on the fact that she will bring a calm to any situation, rather than exacerbating a situation or interaction. When a husband knows his wife will be like a sponge dampening the fires of emotion and argumentation that may exist in a situation, he is more attracted to her. When he knows he can bring his raw emotions and passion to her, and she will not increase the emotion in the room through her reaction, he has found a beautiful woman. A wife who can be the place of calm and harmony in the midst of the storm is indeed a remarkably beautiful woman.

David was called upon to sing soothing songs to the enraged and demonically oppressed King Saul. What David did in those situations conveys this very idea of a positive, quiet spirit. He added something to Saul's life that was invaluable—harmony, calm, and tranquility. Notice that it was not that David just didn't get in the way or didn't say anything... David added something that wasn't there before. He added tranquility and peace (1 Samuel 16:23).

Sometimes a quiet spirit is portrayed as though it is meant to be quiet all the time. This is a gross misapplication of the concept based upon its English translation. A quiet spirit means, "to add something that is extremely valuable and magnetic in its drawing power." When you are around a person with a biblical, quiet spirit, they add something new to you—harmony, encouragement, calm, and clarity.

## Marriage Exercise #6

## Attractive Soul: Quiet Spirit

### *Promoting Positive Harmony and Peace*

The quiet spirit is a positive addition to another's life that produces harmony, peace, encouragement, and the ability to see problems in perspective. To what degree do you have a quiet spirit? Answer the following questions to assess this.

1.  In what ways have you been the opposite of a quiet spirit in your marriage? Look at the following examples: stirring up conflict, increasing emotion, subtracting harmony, adding to confusion, and so on.

2.  How have you been selfish, angry, and demanding in the last month?

3.  How have you added harmony, peace, encouragement, and clarity in your household during the past week? Is this normal for you?

4.  What needs to be added to your husband's life and marriage that will bring him harmony and peace?

5.  How can those things be added? What can you do? Are there other people that can add those things?

## Physical Attractiveness

Warning! This is an area that must be handled with extreme caution. Our purpose in this book is to understand a man's heart so that you can make effective changes in your marriage. We do not want to come across as judgmental or hurtful, so please take these words with an open heart and prayerfully seek how God wants you to use them.

Many women have resisted the suggestion that remaining attractive is one of their husband's top internal needs. They believe that this makes them objects rather than people. Now it is true that the ranking of the top needs men want from their wives can change from man to man, but it is surprising how often "staying attractive" ranks in the top ten things that keep men satisfied and bonded to their wives.

## What does physical attractiveness mean?

Being physically attractive doesn't mean movie star looks. It simply means that an extra effort is being made to make it easier to be with you—applying deodorant, brushing your teeth, showering, combing hair, shaving, wearing clean and attractive clothing, exercising, and eating a healthy diet. These all say to other people, "I like people to enjoy being around me." If we are not willing to say that to our spouse, we are in trouble. We want to be around this type of person all the time and in an intimate way.

This chapter is a very hard chapter to write because it may seem like we are heaping a whole new layer of guilt on women who feel bad already because the culture says they are not beautiful enough. But I have found that men are not expecting their wives to be the perfect definition of beauty by the world's standard. They just need their wives to be beautiful by their standards, which are usually much more generous and broad than the unrealistic ideals of the fashion, cosmetics, or movie industries.

Beauty is more than just what you look like. Your attitude and your character and your personality are key factors in your beauty. It is possible to have a woman with all the right physical features, but she is not as attractive as a woman with the right hidden person of the heart. For example, Linda was overweight, and her husband left her for a woman more overweight because the other woman's attitude was much better. There are scores of women who are beautiful externally but lose their husbands to less "attractive" women because the other woman is more beautiful in a deeper, richer way.

There are two aspects of beauty that must be discussed: First, beauty is enhanced or confirmed by attitude, personality, and character. Second, a wife needs to be attractive to her husband, not to other women or men. First Timothy 2:9, 10 says, "Likewise, I want women to adorn themselves with proper clothing, modestly and discreetly, not with braided hair and gold or pearls or costly garments, but rather by means of good works, as is proper for women making a claim to godliness."

Notice in the Scripture that there is the issue of modesty. A godly woman does not want to dress in such a way that she is a distraction to other men. How a woman dresses should be flattering and appropriate for the situation. She wants to be attractive to her husband but not a temptation to other men through provocative or sensual clothing.

I don't mean to imply that men do not understand real love if they are so fixated on looks. Men are capable of understanding and participating in real, deep, and interactive love. However, God has wired a large percentage of men to be visually stimulated. It is this visual stimulation that acts as a doorway or passage through which deep and intimate love is directed and pursued.

Solomon calls his fiancé "[O] most beautiful among women," and he finds in her the level of beauty and allure that captivates his heart (Song of Solomon 1:8). He has just made a list of why she is not beautiful by the world's standards, but to him she is gorgeous. He gives her the title "Most beautiful among women," and says,

"How beautiful you are, my darling, How beautiful you are!" (1:15). This title is one that all men can and should give to their wives. In fact, when a man agrees to marry a woman, this is the title that he bestows on her. A man's wife is the only woman he can enjoy complete physical intimacy without guilt, so to him she is the definition of beauty. He longs for her to remain beautiful and not allow herself to become less than she really is or was. Clearly, a husband finds in her all the beauty that he needs and wants. It is this element that a wife should be after—a captivated husband, not the adoring adulation of the world.

Listen to Solomon describe what the beauty of a spouse does to a man: "You have made my heart beat faster, my sister, *my* bride; You have made my heart beat faster with a single *glance* of your eyes, With a single strand of your necklace. How beautiful is your love, my sister, *my* bride!" In various parts of the Song of Solomon he praised eight parts of his bride's body: her eyes, hair, teeth, lips, mouth, temples, neck, and breasts. Compared with this lavish praise of the beloved's beauty, some wives today may feel uncomfortable about their own appearance. However, one must remember that initially the daughters of Jerusalem did not seem to regard the beloved as a beautiful woman. Unlike the other royal ladies, she was not fair-skinned – a preeminent sign of beauty in the ancient world (see 1:5, 6). Yet in her lover's eyes she was *beautiful* even though she did not meet the objective standards of beauty in her society.

In other words, though few people in any age meet their own particular culture's standard of beauty, a woman is beautiful in the eyes of her lover simply because he loves her. Every husband who genuinely loves his wife can say, "To me you are beautiful and there is no flaw in you."[2]

## Risks of Letting Yourself Go Physically

If a woman is not willing to work on her side of the marriage, then she is not in a position to leverage change in her husband. Working hard on remaining attractive is involved and difficult and does require discipline. It is much easier to just be functional and driven to accomplish the tasks that she has been given than to also worry about her physical appearance. One of the most difficult things to do for both husbands and wives is to get them to realize that even though they do not have a particular need, their spouse does, and that is why God directs you to meet their needs. This is the work of marriage—to meet the deepest needs of the other person. We are to fill them up in the ways that we are supposed to as their spouse.

Some women do let themselves go physically, but it's likely that their soul dropped its leaves long before the external attractiveness departs. In fact, internal soul changes precede external changes almost every time. Most men just want their wives to be somewhere near the level of attractiveness they had when they dated. Yet some women completely let themselves go after being married for a while or after the first child comes along.

This is where the marriage contract comes into play. She expects him to work and bring home a paycheck, to honor her, to help care for the children, and so on. He expects that she will continue to work hard to keep herself looking nice.

Psychologist Dr. Willard Harley has encountered this problem many times in marriage counseling and has a standard reply:

"You want to be loved for who you are and not for what you do. We all do. But it doesn't work that way. You didn't decide to marry your husband for who he is, but rather for what he did. If he had not met any of your emotional needs when you dated him, you would not have even considered him as a life partner. And if after you were married, he stopped meeting your needs, your feelings for him would have changed considerably. Your love would have simply faded away.

A man with a need for an attractive spouse feels good whenever he looks at his attractive wife. In fact, that's what emotional needs are all about. When one of his emotional needs is met he feels fulfilled, and when it's not met he feels frustrated. It may sound immature or superficial, but I've found that most men have a need for an attractive wife."[3]

Without meaning to, some wives save their worst attitudes and worst looks for their husbands. It seems as though they figure that he just has to understand. "After all, he is my husband," she says. "I have had a really hard day and I don't have time to make myself pretty for him like when we were dating." It is this *I-am-on-to-and-into-other-things* attitude that expands the growing distance between a husband and wife. It becomes clear to a husband whether or not she is still trying to impress him, or if she has begun to take him for granted.

If you want a great marriage, then from your side you are going to have act like you are still trying to win his heart. He was attracted to your beauty. He found a beautiful flower that was willing to bloom for him. Some women think, *He does not doll himself up for me, so why should I for him?* He actually does; he just does it in other ways. He works hard to provide a financial income stream, oftentimes enduring assignments and situations that are unpleasant and difficult. This is his dolling himself up for you.

Dana remembers how her mom would look grungy all day while cleaning the house or other involvements; but every day without fail, she managed to get a bath, put on her makeup, and be dressed beautifully by the time her dad walked through the door. She wanted him to see his pretty wife when he came home.

I've heard other women say the opposite, as in the example of Beth. Beth had been slowly losing her husband, Rob, over twenty years as her weight ballooned. He increasingly avoided her by working, staying out in the garage, or connecting with friends. "If he were a good Christian, he should just accept me as I am," Beth exploded through tears and anger. "I have tried everything; I just can't lose the weight. It just won't come off." In talking with Rob, I learned that it was not so much the weight as the fact that she has just given up on any kind of discipline in that area. "She has convinced herself that she can't, so she doesn't even try." Beth argues, "I know I have put on a few pounds, and I am no longer attractive to him; but don't you think that he should love me anyway? Shouldn't he love the 'me' inside my body, not just my physical shape?" The truth was that the way she looked repulsed him, but her lack of effort repelled him more. He would stay married, but he did not have to like it or pretend that it was OK. He just needed her to take steps toward working on her health and body.

Marlene was a mystery to her husband. When she wanted to, she could be clearly one of the most attractive women he had ever met. But she could also go out in public looking like a homeless person or a bag lady. This deeply troubled and frustrated him. She let herself go sometimes (no hairstyle, no makeup, scruffy clothes, and an abrasive manner), then all of a sudden she would dress to impress and she was gorgeous! He just never knew which Marlene he was going to get.

Sandra was losing her husband, Ken. He was increasingly dissatisfied with her and their marriage. He told her that their marriage was over, and he had already rented an apartment near his work. He flirted with several of the young ladies in his office. To him, he was taking what seemed to be the appropriate action. Sandra had hoped that his love for their two boys would keep him connected to her, but in his mind loving his boys did not mean staying together with their mother. She was changing and he didn't like the changes, so he started making plans for her to no longer be in his life. As she got busier and busier, she began to adopt a more functional appearance because it was easier. He loved his boys, but she was no longer drawing him towards her.

We can debate whether he should have done what he did, but he was clearly not sensing that she loved him. He thought, "If you do not appear interested in attracting or impressing me when we are together, then you do not love me." Sandra decided to try and win him back before she allowed him to throw away their seven years together and the two children. What caught his attention the most was that she began to dress the way he liked and wore her hair and makeup specifically the way he liked it. He couldn't help but notice that the woman he had fallen in love with years before was back. She was just as beautiful and captivating to him now as she was so many years ago when she emerged from beneath the frazzled housewife look. It took extra work that the functional look did not require, but it was a small price to pay for keeping her marriage and family intact.

Let me hasten to add that in our day and age some people are looking for all their needs to be met by their spouse—this is ridiculous. There are nine relationships in our life, only one of which is our marriage. It takes good connections in all the relationships to live a full life. Work hard on your marriage, but realize that it is the whole of life that will build a thoroughly satisfying life.

## Marriage Exercise #7

## Maintaining Physical Attractiveness

1.  What practical ways can I become more attractive physically to my husband? (Evaluate each area and decide if you could improve here.)

    | | | |
    |---|---|---|
    | Colors | Make-up | Friends |
    | Style | Communication | Smile |
    | Clothing | Personality | Touching |
    | Weight | Attitude | Tone of voice |
    | Hair | Mannerisms | Activity level |

2.  What colors does my husband like to see me in?

3.  Is there anything he just hates in my wardrobe?

4.  What kind of hairstyle is most appropriate to him?

5.  Do my friends influence me negatively based on what I know he likes?

6.  What changes are needed in the above areas this week?

# Overemphasis on Hair, Clothes, and Jewelry

The Bible and our culture suggest that it is possible for a woman to focus her self-worth and beauty on externals exclusively. This is always a mistake. A woman's worth is not measured by the kind of jewelry she wears or the style of her hair; it comes from the beauty of her soul. If a woman's soul is beautiful, it allows her to create and sustain life-giving relationships. Her physical beauty may be initially alluring, but this will fade in importance if her soul is selfish, angry, and demanding.

We have all watched as beautiful movie stars marry and divorce, wandering away to another beautiful looking person. These people's external beauty did not fade, but their ability to successfully cover up the selfishness of their soul is gone. They get divorced because there is no love, only external attractiveness. They are really looking for the person with the beautiful soul, which can be hard to find in that environment. It is very hard to maintain a relationship with a person who has a beautiful appearance but is ugly on the inside.

The consistent point that Scripture makes is that a woman should not put too much emphasis on hair, clothing, jewelry; but should be a beautiful person who is gracious, flexible, kind, and caring. It doesn't say that women shouldn't put effort into this area, but that this should not be the major focus of their life. When a beautiful woman is beautiful for her husband, she is directed towards her husband, not competing with other women or for the attentions of men.

## Marriage Exercise #8

### Overemphasis on External Beauty

*What would an excessive level of attention to hair, jewelry, and clothing look like to you?*

*What would inattention to hair, jewelry, and clothing look like?*

*Are you moving toward either of these extremes?*

# Warning: Using Physical Attractiveness Against Your Marriage

A wife's beauty is for strengthening her marriage, yet some women use their physical beauty for more than what it was intended. They seek to allure men outside their marriage to notice and attend to them. Years ago I was asked to counsel two different couples within the same year that dissolved into separation, bitterness, financial devastation, and eventual divorce. Both of the women's friends and associates convinced them that they were too beautiful to stay faithful to just one man for their whole lives. Both ladies were reaching their 40th birthdays and became convinced that soon their beauty would begin to fade. They thought if they ever were to have a fling, now would be the time.

No matter how much arguing or counseling these ladies heard, they would not be convinced that beauty should not be used for selfish pleasure. They used their beauty not for the joy of married love but instead to seduce other men and experience the "joy" of an affair. It didn't work out. It never does. It destroyed their marriages and filled them with guilt and shame. After the multiple affairs had run their course and the beauty they once had was used up by the vile men who took advantage of them, both of their children hated their mothers and told them to their faces. I remember watching one of the ladies try and cuddle up to her children only to have her son shoot an icy look of utter disgust at her as he backed away. The mother turned to me with deep sadness and asked, "How do I get them to love me again?" I told her that I was not sure that she could, "You abandoned them and their father at a crucial moment. You sowed the wind and now you are reaping the whirlwind."

These women damaged their children irreparably. In one case, her two lovely daughters were sent into a tailspin they will never recover from. If their mom could do that, then there was nothing to believe in and nothing was sure. They thought that they might as well throw caution to the wind and sin with a high hand just like their mom. Both of these adulterous ladies ended up living lonely lives, alienated from their children they had spent so many years raising. If they had just listened to the cautions in their own heart and from others, using their gift of beauty for righteous purposes and not sin, they would have enjoyed the undying love and financial support of their husbands, the continued warmth and love of their children, and avoided the seamier, painful side of life.

Even though during their marriages these ladies captivated their husbands by their beauty and built strong and loving families and a secure life, they believed the lie that beauty must be used before it slips away. It is a shame. The Bible is clear in this regard, "Charm is deceitful and beauty is vain, but a woman who fears the Lord she shall be greatly praised" (Proverbs 31:30). Be attractive for your spouse, not for others. Be attractive for the one you have committed to spend your life with. Do not use your beauty for sin and selfishness and betrayal. It will reap a crop that you will wish you hadn't sown.

## Marriage Exercise #9

### Using Your Beauty

If a woman does not use her beauty and femininity to build a deep relationship with her husband, then she has missed the point of the beauty God gave her. What are you using your physical beauty to accomplish?

*Impress your girlfriends?*

*Finding worth by your ability to attract other men?*

*Attaining a higher position on the hierarchy of importance or power?*

*Drawing your husband toward his marriage?*

*Increasing your ability to capture your husband's attention to help him reach his maximum potential?*

## Marriage Exercise #9

## Outer Beauty Considerations

### Hair

The Bible says that the crown of a woman is her hair. Is your hair a good-looking crown or more of a matted-down gunnysack? Most men have a few hairstyles they like to see their wife wear. Consider the following and whether a change needs to be made.

*Style of cut*

*Length*

*Color*

*Shading*

### Weight

How close are you to what you weighed when you got married? Is your weight becoming a health issue? Is your husband concerned about your weight?

Weight control is not complicated—it is just hard work. Eat healthier, eat less, and move more are the only three ingredients that will change what you weigh. If you try and only change one of the three, it is harder to change your weight. If you change all three, you will see results. Many women use food as a medication for negative feelings or to fill wounds. Many women use food as the number one reward for accomplishments. Most people's weight issues are more about their emotional attachments to food than how much they eat. They need to understand what connections they have made with and to food.

## Clothing

*Who do you dress for—yourself, other women, men?*

*Do you consider your dress modest?*

*When was the last time you updated your wardrobe?*

*What are your husband's tastes in clothing? Are these reflected in your wardrobe?*

*Does your wardrobe stimulate your husband?*

## Warning: Don't Give into Bizarre Forms of "Attractiveness"

A woman cannot and should not give into her husbands' fantasies and perverted desires for her to look like a porn star. Because of the prevalence of sexual material, men can begin to think that the huge hair, big lips, and overdone makeup is a desirable look for women. A woman's beauty should be about the radiance of her virtue and not about becoming a sexual object for her husband's pleasure.

# Chapter 9

## Listening

*1 Peter 3:3, 4; 1 Timothy 3:11*

When Susan got married she was absolutely convinced that her husband was the ideal man for her. He was everything she needed and wanted in a man. As their marriage went along, she discovered that he had some serious flaws and problems. For example, she found it increasingly difficult to listen to her husband drone on and on about work, about some friend, or an obstacle he was facing. It was mind numbing to her. It became impossible for her to listen to him say the same things every day—the same problems, the same people, the same situations. He was a good man, but she was increasingly shutting down when he talked.

Susan came to see me so I could talk to her husband and give her tips about how to improve her marriage. She was confident that he was the problem. Instead, we discovered that Susan was a lousy listener. She would derail a conversation she was not interested in so she could talk about something else. She would give signals—yawning, checking her watch, watching TV, fidgeting, and so on—to let him know she was bored with the conversation. She seemed to hope that he would stop talking and ask her questions about herself instead. Her inability to listen to her husband was slowly destroying her marriage.

After a while, I needed to confront her with the fact that she was being selfish and that if she wanted a good marriage, she would need to become a better listener. Luckily, she indicated she wanted to have a great marriage and was willing to learn. I began to teach her the principles of good listening. We invited a friend of hers to attend these classes so she could practice good listening skills before trying them on her husband. It took a while, but she learned to listen to her husband and it saved their marriage. Today, she and her husband enjoy each other as soul mates, having learned how to listen to one another in depth. They discovered that both of them needed different kinds of listening skills from the other, and they each liked to talk about different things. With new skills and lots of practice, this marriage we thought was headed toward "irreconcilable differences" became an enduring success.

## Biblical Understanding of the Need to Listen

We discussed in the previous chapter the idea that a beautiful woman possesses both a quiet and gentle spirit. This ties in perfectly with the concept of being a good listener to your husband – a need that runs so deep he is tempted to betray all he holds dear just to have someone listen to him. The word translated *quiet* in 1 Peter 3:4 is the Greek word *hesuchios*, which means quiet, tranquility, peaceful. It describes someone with a quiet and peaceful state of mind.

The godly wife with a gentle spirit has the ability to not be bothered by the actions of others and the disasters or trouble around them. Such a person has a source of tranquility that is independent of the circumstances they find themselves in. They are able to put a spiritual, mental, and emotional gap between an individual's situation and what they are feeling and thinking inside. They do not allow the emotions, poor choices, and forceful energy of another person to disrupt or mandate who they are or how they feel. Someone with a quiet spirit does not react to the emotions of another but allows them to feel what they feel without demanding a response. They realize that the other person will change their emotions many times each day. They are a sponge putting out the sparks that fly from the other person.

Learning to listening effectively is a major key to a happy and successful marriage. A husband often feels as though he has no one who will really listen to him or allow him to explain his point of view or actions. He longs for and is drawn toward anyone, especially a woman, who will provide that function for him. In fact, he deeply desires to have the one woman closest to him (his wife) provide this often difficult task.

One of the most challenging things about being a wife is listening to your husband explain how he would like to move the family, quit his job, kill his boss, or do bizarre things. But God calls the godly wife to perform this role, and she can only do it if she has the quiet spirit we've described. She does not have to agree with him, but she can draw him to her, gain immense influence in his life, and save him from trouble if she learns this specialized skill. It is similar to becoming a sort of confessor for him, allowing him to vent and spill, sort things out without action behind them. Listening in this way drains off the poison in her husband's life.

In order for her to perform this function, her security, trust, and focus must come from a deeper, higher source—God. When she is able to *not* react to things he says or indicates he wants to do, she can be a great help to him. When she does not respond with venom, anger, repulsion, and fear, it will connect them together in ways that she probably has a hard time imagining. It is said that most affairs involve bad sex and good listening. Why do some men pursue mistresses? It is because the mistress listens to him in a detached but active manner that captivates him. He can tell her anything and she won't be shocked. He can tell her the intimate secrets of his heart, and she will listen and follow his train of thought. After it is over, she will still physically love him. That is a seductive and bonding combination.

Your husband's need for you to listen isn't just about conversation; he wants you to listen with an active-detachment. This involves staying on his topic, asking questions, providing insights, letting him talk, and reflecting back what he seems to be feeling and thinking. We will learn more about each of these later in the chapter. The most important thing is to not react to what he is saying or inserting your self into the topic. He doesn't want you to mentally run ahead of where this line of thinking could go. He just needs you to let him get it all out—to be interested in what he is talking about without an emotional expression.

Yes, this is somewhat different from what a woman typically wants out of talking. When women share their feelings, they are ready to act on them. But men often talk about their feelings with no intention to do anything about them. She typically desires a give and take interaction; moving from topic to topic; exploring one another's thoughts, feelings, and ideas. But he just wants her engaged on his stuff. It is much more like a therapy session than a conversation. In a man's perfect world, his wife is his therapist who listens, asks questions, and helps him work through the things that swirl around in his mind, as if what he says is not going to affect her world.

## Becoming a Great Listener

One of the wonders of a wife who learns to listen well is that she exerts far more influence in her husband's life than any other person. She has access to the inner avenues of his mind and heart. A small suggestion made in the depth of his soul by a trusted friend can change behavior quickly. Many women want to know the secret to changing their husband. One of the secrets is listening to him deeply without reaction. This seems like the opposite of what would cause him to change. But becoming his most trusted confidante, and the person he feels safe to open his heart to, allows you to point out areas of concern and needed change. By listening well, he will be drawn to you and need you in ways that will change both of your lives.

Most women long for an intimate marriage but do not realize that they instinctively listen in a way that ensures this will never happen. Most wives react to what their husband is thinking or feeling because they fear how it could directly impact them. If he talks about wanting to quit his job because the boss is a bear, it is hard for her to shut down her feelings and just enter into his topic, allowing him to express his thoughts and feelings without running on ahead in her mind. Everyone thinks and feels things that they will never do or say. He is looking for someone safe enough to hear it and not jump to the conclusion that he would act on it. If a wife does not learn to listen with active detachment, he will come to realize that she is not a safe person to open up to. He will not share who he really is with her.

Think of a time when you had a conversation with someone who constantly disagreed with everything you said. It's probable that a deep conversation was not possible because you probably didn't feel totally heard. It's the same for your husband. In order to listen to his soul, he must be allowed to expose the thoughts and feelings he has without fear of embarrassment, disagreement, and arguing. There will be time later for correction or comment. Good listeners are not about the accuracy of what the person is saying but about hearing what the person means to say.

Our culture is multiplying counselors and psychologists because no one but paid professionals know how to listen without reaction. A man wants his wife to be this special type of confidante who can hear all about who he really is—his insecurities, his fears, his fantasies, his dreams, his scars, and so on. In order to be a good listener, you must maintain emotional distance between you and the topic of conversation. If you get pulled into your husband's emotions or react to his topic, then you are really not listening well and usually he will stop talking. You must maintain an emotional gap between you and him. You must hear what he is saying and feeling, realizing that he has a right to express them even though they are not necessarily true. You are permitting him to give his opinions and perspectives without judgment.

One of the most difficult assignments a wife can accept is the development of her soul to the point where nothing anyone can say will cause her to react. Instead, she will allow the person to emote and even rant while staying actively detached from what the other person is saying. By the way, this works really well on teenagers too.

When you are listening to the depths of someone's soul, realize that there are a lot of thoughts, fantasies, and hidden actions that are not nice and pretty. You have to constantly remind yourself about the *overall* actions of the person, as well as their individual worth before God as a human. Do not take the statements, feelings, or thoughts of your husband as action items in his to-do list. He needs someone who understands that he thinks about a lot of things he won't act on. Active-detached listening is a life-long learning assignment.

My wife, Dana, writes, "I think it's so much easier to listen to a girlfriend than my husband. What she says doesn't affect me, so she can say what she wants and I am happy to listen. I need to constantly remind myself to detach my feelings and just listen to Gil like I do to my girlfriends."

I (Gil) eventually set up classes at church for women to learn how to listen to their husbands without reacting. The classes drew many women. They learned that when they are listening, what they feel is irrelevant. He needs to feel safe with his wife and for her to be engaged in what he is saying.

## Risks of Not Listening Well

If a woman will not perform the loving act of listening to her husband, he will simply stop talking about anything important; and the intimacy of the marriage she had hoped would develop will never get off the ground. So she must find a way to be fascinated by his world, his emotions, and his stuff. She can do this by asking questions, probing, following his train of thought, summarizing, and suggesting themes, solutions, and perspectives. In short, she needs to engage in his topics.

Now it is true that many men hide their emotions. It is not always easy to get down to the real man inside, and it is not always pretty when you get in there. It is also true that many wives think they already know what their husband feels and thinks from the brash, loud, or angry statements he makes. Since they assume they already know, they don't persist in drawing out those emotions and forceful opinions. That's when misunderstandings occur and resentment can build. It is impossible to have an intimate marriage if your husband's perspectives, thoughts, opinions, and deep feelings are not being really heard. The rewards that come from deep-level communication are immense. They are worth the risk, the effort, and the time—they make the marriage and life, in general, more satisfying.

Carol dragged her husband to see me for marriage counseling. She was hoping I would fix their marriage as they had been separated numerous times before. Her major complaint was that he would not talk. He was a thoughtful man who found it hard to express his thoughts quickly or easily. He had a slight stutter and a limited vocabulary; but if you took the time to listen, he had some profound things to say. Carol, however, was always finishing his sentences, correcting his comments, and talking for him. Eventually he would just go to the garage and play pool with a few of his buddies. When he had enough of her yelling, nagging, screaming, and constant talking, he would leave for a few weeks. A couple of times he was gone for months. In her mind their marriage problems were about him and his unwillingness to stay committed and talk. She never conceived that she was one of the major problems. She had no idea that her lack of ability to listen was driving a huge wedge through their marriage and threatening to destroy it.

When I suggested that she had a listening problem, her quick mind jumped on the absurdity of that and she rattled on for ten minutes about how that could not be the case. This was going to be a tough sell. Limiting her talking, except to ask questions, was like putting a muzzle on her life; but it was the beginning of a new renaissance in their marriage. John would take three to four times longer than the average person to complete his sentences, but he thought deeply and was willing to share his feelings. Getting Carol to wait for him to finish his sentences; to probe his ideas, plans, and emotions; and to not react to the implications took at least six months. The better she became at listening, the better their marriage worked. The more she asserted her old style, the more withdrawn he became and the more fights they had. He was not always right, but he deeply wanted to be listened to by the woman he had chosen as his bride. When she refused to do that for him, he was not interested in the marriage.

## Marriage Exercise #1

### Active-Detached Listening

The goal of listening is to let your mate communicate who he is. We don't want to kill his desire to expose his soul by reacting to what he says. There is *task* communication, exchanging facts, and there is the communication of your *soul*. In order to meet this deep need of his to be heard and understood, you have to be a safe person so that he will expose his soul to you. You become safe when you listen with active detachment.

1.  Here are suggestions for how to listen with active detachment:

    *Do not react to what he is saying.*

    *Be responsive. He wants to know you are engaged in the conversation.*

    *Remind yourself that these are his ideas and feelings, not necessarily the truth.*

    *Realize you can make suggestions later.*

    *Keep asking questions and probe.*

    *Remember he won't necessarily act on what he says he is going to do.*

2.  It is usually best if you are not the person who shuts down an idea. Find others who suggest that this path is not wise or agree it shouldn't be done.

*When you think of objections to something your husband is saying, keep thinking about whether you can find someone else to say it for you.*

*Be open to the idea that a new direction may be the best course of action. Your husband will likely come up with a new idea that is good.*

## The Problem of Betrayal

The Apostle Paul wrote, "Women must likewise be dignified, not malicious gossips, but temperate, faithful in all things" (1 Timothy 3:11). The word *gossip* is the word *diabolos*, which means, "slanderer, devil-like one." A wife must develop the ability to keep a confidence or her husband will not share with her the deepest secrets of his heart. This is true in life as well. If you want to be intimate with someone, you must know how to keep a confidence. He will stop sharing with you if he hears that what he shares with you is repeated to your friends. You are no longer a safe person.

Some men are so afraid of this breach of etiquette and trust that they forbid their wives from talking about their marriage or what happens in the home in any way. There is a real sense of betrayal when a wife shares the details of what happens in the home—either the things he says or the things done there. Keeping confidences is vital to the relationship as long as what he is saying or doing is not illegal, immoral, or harming you physically, emotionally, or mentally.

## Marriage Exercise #2

## Eliminating Betrayal & Gossip

Most husbands would never share another personal matter with their wives if they knew that their wives had already told other people confidential things about them. If they get any kind of inclination that you are not trustworthy, they will not share their heart again. If you have gossiped about your husband in a negative way, begin by confessing your sin before the Lord and repent.

*Who are you tempted to share intimate details with?*

*Who are the women you know who never say anything bad about their husbands?*

*Are you a slanderer about your husband's faults?*

*Do you have friends who share personal things about their husbands around you? Be careful around these women because they will make it seem acceptable to disrespect your husband and possibly tempt you to join in.*

If you really want to talk about your husband, cover his good points! You can model positive talk of your husband to other wives.

*What are his five greatest strengths?*

*How does he show you he loves you?*

*What great accomplishment has he tackled this week?*

## Why Was It Easier to Listen Before Marriage?

Before a woman commits to a man, she is able to listen to his stories and actions without an emotional investment in what he is saying. She can be objective and remain outside the story. But once they are a couple—and especially after they are married—whatever he does has a direct bearing on her life. It is her ability to listen with a high level of attention and emotional distance that is especially attractive and desired by husbands.

Wives need to learn the secrets of listening well. They need to learn how to listen to things they don't care about and to his wacky ideas, problems, thoughts, and feelings without reacting. When you were dating you may have heard what was being said but told yourself you would change that later. You might have realized that listening to your future husband was the price of getting married to him. You are a wise wife when you realize that what you won him with in the first place is what he is still expecting.

Women often set up a condition that he assumed would continue. Men assume that throughout the days ahead, their wives will listen to them talk about their stuff in the same way they listened during courtship. He still needs someone who can listen to him and help him process things. He may never have agreed to marriage if he had known that his "confidante" was going to lose interest in listening after the wedding.

## Honing Your Listening Skills

Communication is vital to a healthy marriage and requires work by both people. Many couples never take time to actually talk to one another unless there is a big problem. They may throw facts at one another while watching TV or as they are going out to the next activity. This isn't really talking in the way that we mean.

Men typically want to talk about the things they like or are interested in, and they often don't want to talk about things their wives want to talk about.

Most wives really do want an intimate marriage with their husbands where they are married to their soul mate. In order to be a soul mate to another person, you have to regularly listen to their soul and embrace it with gentleness and acceptance. Many wives destroy the very thing they want because they do not know how to overcome their tendency to react too quickly to what their husbands are saying. Practice these skills and you will often discover that you really are married to your soul mate. There are only a few things that cause a husband to want to please his wife, like having a soul mate that listens to the whole of his world.

The following techniques will signal you are really interested in listening to them. They are simple but take practice to use effectively. When mastered, they communicate that the other person is very valuable to you; that you really want to understand what they are thinking and feeling. These are invaluable skills for all healthy relationships.

## Make Eye Contact

Active listening requires looking at the speaker. There is no escaping the fact that looking at the person who is talking facilitates deeper conversation. It tells the speaker, "Keep going, talk more, I'm listening to what you are saying." It lets them know that they are valuable to you. When someone is talking to you, it is natural to instinctively judge the nature of the communication. We show our lack of interest if we look away since it expresses boredom, distraction, and disinterest. Everybody picks up on these non-verbal clues.

Start looking at your husband while he is talking (not staring, just looking at his face while he is talking). This takes practice because you will want to do fifty different things at the same time while you are listening to him—like doing the dishes, watching the TV, reading a magazine, working on chores, taking care of the kids, and so on. But try to resist. Doing those things while he is talking says to him that you are not listening and don't care. You can always ask him to pick up the conversation later if you need a minute to finish something.

I remember one couple I worked with where the wife had a deep desire to really understand her husband, but she also wanted to be as efficient as possible and so sought to do a number of chores while he was talking. She ended up talking all about her day, but he would not open up about his because there was no focused eye contact with him. Until she was willing to stop and actually look at him when he was talking, the level of sharing she had always hoped for could not be realized.

## Marriage Exercise #3

### Making Eye Contact

For one week, try looking at the people who are talking to you. Focus on their face. Put down the book, the newspaper, or magazine; turn off the TV; and look at them. Read all the nonverbal clues from what they are saying. Look for emotion bubbling to the surface in their eyes.

## Positive Body Language

Non-verbal cues (body language) signal to the other person your feelings about what they are saying. We give off body language without knowing it. We do certain things that give off either a positive or negative vibe. When you are interested in what the person is saying, you do several positive cues that express to the other person that you are engaging them. Likewise, there are negative cues that express complete boredom and disinterest that you want them to stop talking.

Positive signals include leaning toward the person, making eye contact, looking at them, or nodding slightly. Negative signals are leaning back, slouching, looking away, fidgeting, or folding your arms. These communicate boredom, disinterest, or even disagreement. During counseling training I was taught to lean in at various points in the conversation to signal to the counselee that I was with them and that what they were saying was valuable. You can force yourself to become more engaged in the conversation by paying attention to your body language.

## Marriage Exercise #4

### Positive Body Language

Take some time to sit across from your husband and ask him questions about work, his favorite sports team, or hobby. Practice positive body signals like leaning towards him while he is talking, to say, "I am interested in you." Be aware when your body language is more negative and consider what it communicates. These habits can be changed and fine-tuned over time.

| Positive Body Language: | Negative Body Language: |
| --- | --- |
| Looking directly at them | Leaning back |
| Leaning forward | Slouching |
| Nodding your head slightly | Wringing hands or fidgeting |
| Making eye contact | Folding your arms |
| Facial gestures, like smiling | Looking around |

## Use Minimal Encouragers

Minimal encouragers are the various grunts, groans, phrases, and expressions that tell another person you want them to keep talking. These vary according to where you live, your culture, background, and age. They don't really mean anything except, "Keep talking; I'm paying attention." Minimal encouragers can also be hand signals, raising your eyebrows, widening the eyes, smiling, positive facial reactions, and tilting the head. These count as other types of body signals that encourage the person to keep talking.

If none of these signals are given, it is extremely difficult to keep talking, especially to go deeper. Some people naturally give out more of these signals, and we think of them as very charismatic and good conversationalists. They make us want to talk with them. Some people are almost aerobic in their encouragement to keep talking, while others are more like blank walls. It is very hard to talk to this kind of person. People attribute all kinds of negative emotions and motives to these blank-expression individuals.

## Marriage Exercise #5

## Using Minimal Encouragers

If you are skilled at listening, you can guide the talker into opening up areas of their life just by using minimal encouragers along with the other listening techniques we discussed. These phrases or expressions may not come naturally to you, but you can practice them and become skilled at helping people talk to you. Pick a few of the phrases below and try saying them over and over until they come out naturally. You can also pick up on phrases and sounds of the people around you. Then in your next conversation with a friend or your husband, purposely inject these encouragers to keep them talking. Add more facial reactions and watch what happens. A few examples:

> *"I hear you."*
> *"No!"*
> *"Well!"*
> *"Fascinating!"*
> *"Really?"*
> *"I don't believe it!"*
> *"You don't say!"*
> *"Oh!"*
> *"Uh-huh."*

## Verbal Following

Verbal following is a very important skill and one that is the least practiced. It requires following the speaker's subject without switching to other subjects based on what his words reminded you of or something else you want to talk about. It is natural for all kinds of ideas to pop into our minds while other people are talking. You will be reminded about something that happened to you or something you wanted to talk with them about. You may have vehement opposition to their perspective that you want to get out or have facts to share that they don't have. All of these are distractors from the job of good listening. The key is to listen, let them talk about what they want to talk about, and let them complete their thoughts.

It is very rare in our day and age for people to actually have anyone fully hear them out on a subject or topic. So we never feel like we are ever really heard. To "verbally follow" another person means that you value them enough to follow them through all the twists and turns of how they think about a subject, even if it doesn't make sense to you.

One of the common complaints that wives make about their husbands is that they want to talk about the same boring old things—work, sports, or hobbies. Wives often have no natural interest in talking about those things. Even so, they have to realize that what he wants to talk about is important and interesting to him or he would not want to talk about it. That is why listening techniques are so important—they can show your husband you love him.

Another problem wives run into is that their husbands don't do anything about the problems they mention every day. This may be true; but if you were to devote a half hour to an hour each day listening to him about his issues, he would be able to think more clearly about them and potentially fix them. You may even be the one to gain the position and influence to suggest solutions and be heard.

## Marriage Exercise #6

## Practice Verbal Following

Mark out an hour for five nights this week in which you will follow your husband on his topics of interest without changing the subject. Really try hard to listen without injecting what you are reminded of or telling him about your day. This will be one of the hardest things you can do. Just focus for one solid hour on his topic—I think you'll find that it will go places you may not expect.

Can you keep your husband talking about a subject that interests him for an hour without needing to talk about a subject that interests you during that time? If you can give your husband an hour of verbal following every day, you will be irresistible.

## Asking Questions

Asking questions says, "You are important to me, and I am interested in what you want to talk about." The better you become at asking questions, the more you will find out about others, and the more they will understand you really do care for them.

Focused, non-reactive listening is a crucial skill to develop. It helps business leaders, parents of teens, marriages, conflict situations, and so on. To be able to really hear what the other person is saying opens up the possibility of growth and relationship in new ways. Asking questions is a tool for helping you get there.

When someone is talking to you, instead of thinking about what you will say in response, start formulating questions you can ask to encourage the person to tell you more of what they are thinking. It is amazing how encouraging it is to ask people follow-up questions. Discipline yourself to ask questions that further explore what the other person thinks about a subject. When the subject is depleted, new topics can be brought up. Remember there will be plenty of time later to give your opinion. The most important thing you can say to your mate is "I love you." You say that by listening well.

### Marriage Exercise #7

### Ask Questions

1. The skilled listener asks a lot of questions and doesn't try to make statements. Instead, they seek to continue the conversation, encouraging the other person to open up. To do this, try these tips:

- Focus solely on the other person for the time being. Set aside your own thoughts, opinions, and suggestions.
- Develop an insatiable curiosity about almost everything the other person is talking about.
- Learn to ask questions even about things you think you know the answer to.
- Example of encouraging questions might look like:

  *What are you thinking about?*
  *What are you feeling?*
  *What do you think about _____?*
  *How is _____ doing?*
  *Remember the last time we talked about _____; what happened with that?*
  *Have you had a chance to _____ lately?*

- Avoid reacting negatively to the answers—use active detachment and ask additional questions to continue drawing the person out.
- There will be time to give your opinion, particularly if the person asks, "What do you think?"

2. Most bad ideas will be exposed if you get enough facts or counsel. When you have a hard time not reacting, it is a good idea to ask questions that will get them thinking. Oftentimes this works to help the speaker come to the conclusion that what he is saying is not a good idea. It is much like talking with teenagers who think they know it all. They want you to listen, but they don't want you to react or power up and shut down their thoughts. Note, these questions should not be fired in quick succession or then it seems like an inquisition. Try to be positive and encouraging, taking time to get all the facts. Here are examples of the types of questions you could use:

*Now that is interesting... what made you think of that?*

*I am fascinated by this idea; can you tell me more about that?*

*That is a different kind of idea; can you tell me where you think that will go?*

*That idea has some very good upsides, but it may have some downsides, too. Have you thought about any of those?*

*Help me understand more about this idea?*

*Have you checked with...?*

*Have we heard back from...?*

## Paraphrasing (Reflecting Back)

Paraphrasing (or reflecting back) is a listening technique that is very helpful when people are emotional. It takes a little getting used to, but it works wonders in getting at the root of the emotion. To paraphrase, or reflect back, is to repeat the same words or similar words the person just said. The key to good paraphrasing is to pick out the *emotional words* and say them back to the other person. If your husband says, "This guy really makes me angry!" you might say back, "It sounds like you are angry at this guy!"

Usually, if you reflect back the same emotion they are feeling, they will explain more about it because they think you care and want to understand what they're feeling. Some wives tell me, "But I don't want to know more about it!" Remember, this is an attempt to minister to him; you are not doing it to gain valuable information for yourself. You are helping him to process the feelings and get to the root of the emotion. When he is allowed to emote in a safe environment and sort through his emotions out loud, he can then respond more effectively to the problem or situation.

249

## Marriage Exercise #8

### Paraphrasing

Next time your husband – or even your teenager – comes to you in an emotional state, try to paraphrase that emotion by reflecting it back to them. The idea is to draw out the reason for the emotion and to help them process why they are feeling that way. You are also trying to diffuse the emotion so they can think rationally. For example, when your teenager comes home and says, "I hate school. I just want to quit!" remain calm and then say back, "Wow! You sound really upset." Let him continue while you reflect back until the situation is resolved.

## Summarizing

Good listeners check to see if they heard (understood) what the speaker really meant to say. After a thought is finished, they will periodically ask something like, "Can I make sure I understood what you just said?" Then they summarize what they thought they heard you say. It works best when these things are summarized in bullet points. For example, "So you are saying that you hate your job because the boss doesn't understand what he is doing; Bill, who works with you, doesn't carry his end of the job. Do I have that right?"

Usually, it is best to mention only three thoughts at a time. You are just checking to see if he meant what he said or if you heard correctly. This usually operates like a minimal encourager—an invitation to talk more. It is also an invitation to go deeper on a subject. Your husband might say, "No! That is not what I meant to say," when that is exactly what he said; but having heard it, he realizes it is not what he intended. Don't correct him; instead, let him change what he said and explore deeper into his thoughts and feelings.

In many cases a good listener allows a person to express things that they have not even realized they felt before. It may be new territory for the person speaking, so don't hold them to the exact meaning of the words they first used. Give them a chance to clarify, to go deeper, and to think out loud. A wife who really loves her husband will allow him to express opinions he is just thinking about.

## Marriage Exercise #9

### Summarizing

Next time your husband wants to discuss something that is important to him, practice the summarizing technique. It could be that he is trying to process an idea, a problem, or find a solution to something. When he finishes a thought, ask him, "Let me see if I understand what you're saying..." and then follow with two to three bullet points—thoughts about what you think he meant. Let him continue talking once you are sure you understand.

## Listening in Your Marriage

It takes time to develop the listening skills mentioned above, but they are a worthwhile investment of your time and energy. Once you've mastered a few of them, I'm confident you will see a remarkable difference in the quality and depth of your relationships. Since our focus is on bettering the relationship with your husband, let's take a look at ways to make listening work in your marriage.

## Maintain Emotional Distance

Maintaining emotional distance is not easy when what the other person is saying has clear implications for you. A wife needs to develop the art of being very interested in her husband while he is speaking without running out the obvious possible conclusions in her mind. She must maintain emotional distance from what he is talking about or she will not make a good listener and will never be invited into her husband's soul.

## Focus your Attention on Listening

When it's time to listen, stop everything and focus your attention on him. All of us have been forced to listen to a spouse who says things that, if they were to happen, would have a huge impact on our life. All he needs is for you to listen and not react. Since I'm sure you have done this at least once in your life, it is important to cultivate this ability to listen without reacting, which requires your full attention. Put down the book, turn off the TV, stop wiping the counter, and take advantage of the opportunity to just listen.

## Discuss Reactions Later

Write down any strong reactions you may want to address after you have finished listening to your husband. Usually, you would not show him this written reaction because it might not accurately express your actual reactions and thoughts. It is important that you have reaction time, but it should not be in conjunction with your focused time of listening to your husband. We suggest a rule that we use in our house: *the two-hour/two-day rule.* This means that if one of us is really emotional about something the other person said or did, we wait two hours or two days to calm down before we bring it up. It is important that you allow the emotions to be drained out of the issue before you try and resolve it. Many times it takes a number of hours, or even a number of days, to be rational about certain topics. You want to hear the other person's point of view without becoming emotional to the point that you become angry, withdrawn, or unable to present your position.

## Undistracted Listening Times

Every marriage needs to find regular times and ways of having undistracted listening and conversation. A husband needs this and so does a wife. The following suggestions might work for you and your husband, although you probably can come up with ideas of your own. Each individual and marriage is different.

**Changing clothes.** Set aside a half-hour as soon as you or your husband gets home to talk in the bedroom. Often one or both parties need to change clothes to get ready for activities at home. Extend this time to include some focused attention. If your husband has a tendency to rush out, slow him down with some questions and see if he will engage in talking while the ideas and interactions are still fresh.

**Taking walks.** Many couples have found that if they take a walk together in the morning or evening, it allows them undistracted time to talk. I remember a couple that lived on the street I grew up on who took a walk every evening. They were deeply engaged in conversation as they went past our house. This can be a great way of getting both husband and wife away from the distractions around the house. Even when the children are small, they can be pushed in strollers or ride bikes and so on. "Gil and I have been taking walks several times per week," Dana says. "I love this time. I can listen, focus, and follow his topic without distraction from the children, the housework, or the phone."

**Right after dinner**. In our culture, having a conversation right after the evening meal has become a forgotten art, but it can be quite effective. Find an opportunity to plan a dinner where everyone in the family can sit down together. Don't rush to the next activity or jump to the next chore. Try to schedule dinner early enough so that the kids don't have to go to their activity right after the last bite is consumed. Some wives have found it appropriate to dismiss the kids to go do the dishes or homework and then begin engaging her husband more about his day.

## Minimize Distractions

Minimize distractions by picking a consistent time to talk every day. It is helpful to get into the routine of talking about the same time every day so that everyone in the family expects it. There needs to be a daily routine that includes talking and a weekly routine that includes talking *and* focused listening. It is true that some days will not work because of scheduling conflicts, but a few days are better than no days.

Also, if conversation takes place in the same place, it helps. It is helpful if both husband and wife find the place comfortable and distraction-free. Make sure that if you are going after deep conversation, you do not try and do it with the TV or radio on. Even if you can get started with these things playing in the background, they will likely distract or derail the conversation at some point in time. Eliminate this distraction at the beginning because it could be crushing to the conversation later.

## Sobering Issues

The Scriptures ask women repeatedly to be sober. As this pertains to listening, it means, "Do not become drunk emotionally with what is being said. Create some distance between what your husband says and what he will actually do." It can be difficult for women to listen with the two attributes that a man most needs out of listening: active and detached. Active, because he wants her to be interested and alive to the topic that he is discussing. Detached, so she does not immediately react to his ideas and plans. If she races ahead in her thoughts and cannot learn to leave the implications of what he is saying until later, she will not be a good listener; and she will not be meeting this need in him.

There are very few things a woman can do that is as rewarding to her husband as listening with focused, detached attention. It is a rare man that has a wife who pays attention to his verbal wanderings. As I said before, most affairs are really about bad sex and good listening. A man needs, and often craves, a woman to pay attention and listen. I know many women who say they would love it if their husbands would just talk to them. But often their idea of talking and his idea of talking are two different things. In fact, many women act in ways that ensure her husband will never open up like she wants him to or in the way he needs to.

If a man opens up, he will only repeatedly do so if he senses the environment is safe, and the person he is talking to can remain personally objective about the information he is trying to share. Getting him to open up requires that you:

*Probe with him on the journey into his thoughts without prejudice and pretense.*

*Allow him to hold erroneous views on things and not feel the need to correct him.*

*Don't run through the personal implications of what he saying in your mind.*

*Listen for his expression of emotions in order to probe further.*

255

*Refuse to use what you learn in a manipulative way.*

If a wife changes the subject to her topic, interrupts before he completes his thoughts, or expresses boredom about his interests, topics, or ideas, then she is not safe person and the intimacy she seeks is in jeopardy. She must remain "sober" or emotionally distant from what he is saying even though it may have a direct and immediate impact on her life. That is why this is one of the harder needs to meet.

Just remember that a man will be irresistibly drawn to a woman who allows him to tell his story, no matter how convoluted, contrived, and masculine it is. There is something in a man's makeup that revels in telling a woman—mainly his woman—all about his life. He wants her to know how hard it is, what he has to put up with, the challenges he faces, and what he sacrifices every day. It is often hard for a woman to hear it because she can see with incredible clarity that his choices and actions are the cause of his difficulties. But that kind of clarity will not draw him to her or give him the ability to change. A man changes in the direction of the one who accepts him and allows him to be who he thinks he is.

## Warning: Hearing Disturbing Things

A woman cannot, and should not, listen to her husband's detailed descriptions of sin, perversion, or wickedness. Some men use a women's desire to listen to desensitize them to the depths of depravity. While it is important that your husband feel safe to share with you what he is feeling, you do not need to listen to his detailed description of sexual perversion or violent mayhem. Sometimes a man will glory in the details of these sins so that his wife will be more open to allowing him to act this way or be less shocked when he does something less evil.

# Conclusion

What we have been talking about in this book is in essence a job description for married women. These are things to work on to maximize their ability to be on a winning team. This is about how to build credibility and say the things to help the marriage succeed. Most people want to be on winning teams, but they are unwilling to admit that they may be one of the key reasons why their team doesn't win. If you want your marriage to win, your husband must win.

Now there may be evil husbands who destroy almost any possibility of developing a winning marriage; but by far, the vast majority of husbands are regular guys who will come out of their chair in gratitude and willingness to change for the wife who does what we have talked about in this book. Try not to put your head in the sand and believe that everything is his fault to avoid having to change yourself. Even if you think he is 70 percent of the problem, you should do what God's Word says a wife should do. It is often just the simple act of one person fulfilling their God-given role that provides the energy to get a marriage moving forward again.

## Beth's Story—She Chose to Fight

Beth is a legend in her church and family. She saved her marriage. Rob, her husband, began an affair with a younger woman who worked at a local business their family patronized. Rob announced that he was going to leave Beth and their three children to marry his girlfriend. A number of people in the church confronted Rob and prayed for Beth, but there seemed to be nothing that would change his mind. I had a meeting with Beth where I said, "You have basically two options: you can let him go on with his plan and be done with his adulterous, hurtful, and manipulative ways, or you can fight for your husband."

Beth chose to fight for the future of her family and for her husband. She began an intensive learning curve in this book about the seven needs of a husband. She made sure she was better able to meet her husband's needs than this young lady. Rob thought it was great to have two women competing for his attention. Beth had many prayer warriors praying for her and for him that he would come to his senses. She also confronted the young woman and told her Rob was still married and she needed to stop seeing her husband.

Beth informed Rob's employer that Rob was having an affair and threatening to leave his three young children. She also told the young woman's employer that an employee had seduced her husband while he was a client. Beth created an environment in which it was very difficult to pursue the affair and made it easy for Rob to come back to her. In a short period of time the choice became obvious to Rob. His wife, Beth, really loved him and knew how to meet his deepest needs. She was also the mother of his three children. The other woman meant financial ruin, separation from his kids, an uphill battle to see each other, and the condemnation of his friends, colleagues, and employer. She did not meet as many of his needs as his wife now did. He chose his wife. After they got back together, I had the opportunity to teach Rob how to meet Beth's deepest relational needs. Together they are building a marriage of great joy.

A man marries a particular woman because he believes that she will consistently meet these needs in his life. He sees an endless involvement with this particular woman who can meet his unique marital needs. He would not get married if he thought that after six months to a year she would stop meeting them and wander off to pursue her own needs. The work of marriage for a wife is to keep meeting her husband's needs after the fun, ease, and joy of courting is over. If you want your marriage to work at a new level, you must meet these needs. If you want to gain the leverage to help your husband reach his full potential and eliminate a few of his annoying habits, meet these needs. Meeting these needs is a means to an end—the work of a marriage relationship from the woman's side.

## Regina's Story—A Godly Wife

Regina is a legend in her church, in her community, and in her husband's heart. When I think about a woman who single handedly built a marriage of great joy, I think of this woman. She and her husband are now older, but the joy that still emanates from their marriage is amazing. When you are around them, you get the feeling that they are having a great time – both publically and privately. It is plain to see that it is not because of him, although he is a good man. It is her actions. She embraced the wife role as one of the most significant roles of her life. She meets his needs, and they have a continuing fountain of joy bubbling out of their life together. It is a joy to watch her.

In every community and in every church, there is at least one woman like this. It is not because of her beauty or her personality, but it is because she has embraced the requirements of the wife's role and ministered to her husband. Women like this do not only focus on being a wife—they are mothers, Christians, leaders, volunteers, workers, and so on. But they understand that their marriage is a huge part of their life and they have responsibilities in that relationship. It is their full embrace of the role and duties of a wife that allows them to enjoy a marriage of great joy.

## Picture the Awful Wife

One of the easiest ways to see the power of the wife meeting her husband's deepest needs is to reverse the process and ask, "Who would be attracted to an awful wife?" Let's take a look at the awful wife. Few women allow themselves to become this nightmare, but many allow themselves to move in these directions and then wonder why their husband is not interested and engaged in the marriage.

1. The awful wife belittles her husband to others or even to his face in multiple ways by rehearsing his failings, weaknesses, and shortcomings in her mind. Are you like this?

2. The awful wife is demanding and inflexible, refusing to consider that she could be wrong; and in most cases, her opinion and decisions must win. Does this describe you in any way?

3. The awful wife is helpless, lazy, and overspending or is self-focused on career, hobbies, or friends—leaving the home, family, and marriage in disarray. Are you becoming this kind of wife in any of these areas?

4. The awful wife consistently refuses her husband's interest in physical intimacy, making sex a reward for good behavior, or with so little frequency that the man rarely expects to be intimate with her. Are you moving in this direction?

5. The awful wife creates a world full of selfish or feminine pursuits, refusing to converse or participate in any areas that

he enjoys, and often belittles his likes and interests. Does this describe you in any way?

6. The awful wife is quick to complain, is ungrateful, inflexible, critical, demanding, self-centered, bossy, and neglects her physical appearance. Can you improve in this area in specific ways?

7. The awful wife finishes her husband's sentences, changes the subject if it doesn't interest her, is always quick to openly react to what he is saying, and expresses boredom with his topics, feelings, ideas, and concerns. Does this describe you in any way?

Imagine if you were married to a person like this. Would you be attracted to this person? Would you want to exert a lot of energy to make their life better? If we were to ask your husband, would he say that you are beginning to exhibit any of these toxic qualities? If any of these describe you in any way, it is not an accurate excuse to say that he makes you like this. You are choosing to respond to what is around you with these responses. The good news is that you don't have to continue being like that. With God's help, He can help you see where and how to change.

## In Closing

Our purpose in writing this book is to enrich your marriage. These actions are ways for you as a wife to significantly increase the love your husband feels toward you. If done with a gentle and loving nature, it will provide you with the leverage to explain how your husband can meet your needs, and you two can build a deeply enjoyable marriage. As a woman lives out her role of being a radical, godly wife, she will express it differently and with a wonderful uniqueness. These actions that we have suggested for a wife do for her husband are the basic ways that a woman fulfills her side of the marriage relationship.

We realize that this book is packed with a lot of information and that it's easy to feel defeated and overwhelmed. Try to master all of these things but try it over time—not all at once. Like much of life, it's a process. It is not possible to do all of these perfectly right away. It takes time, practice, perseverance, and commitment.

It is more helpful to take all of this in and then prayerfully ask God to put on your heart what quality He would like you to work on. He knows your husband better than you do. Focus on that quality until it feels more natural and comfortable. It may take weeks, months, or even years to fully develop the ability to love your husband in these ways. Take each quality one at a time and be willing to ask your husband about the area that would be the most powerful in his life. Let this be a journey...let God bless you. Trust Him! He made you to be your husband's friend, lover, and closest confidante. He made you to be his wife.

# Notes

## Chapter 3
[1] Dale Carnegie, *How to Win Friends and Influence People* (New York: Simon & Schuster Inc., 1936; renewed 1964; revised 1981).

## Chapter 4
[1] Gary Smalley, *The DNA of Relationships* (Carol Stream, IL: Tyndale, 2004), 49.

## Chapter 5
[1] Willard F. Harley Jr., *His Needs, Her Needs* (Old Tappan, NJ: Fleming H. Revell, 1986), 133-135.

## Chapter 6
[1] Stephen Arterburn, *Every Man's Battle* (Colorado Springs, CO: Waterbrook Press, 2000), 63-64.
[2] At the 2003 meeting of the American Academy of Matrimonial Lawyers, two-thirds of the 350 divorce lawyers who attended said the Internet played a significant role in divorces in the past year, with excessive interest in online porn contributing to more than half of such cases.
http://www.psychologytoday.com/blog/inside-porn-addiction/201112/is-porn-really-destroying-500000-marriages-annually. Last Accessed January 17, 2014.

## Chapter 8

[1] W. Vine and F. Bruce, *Vine's Expository Dictionary of Old and New Testament Words, Vol. 2* (Old Tappan, NJ: Revell, 1981), 1-242 (published in electronic form by Logos Research Systems, 1996).

[2] Dallas Theological Seminary faculty, *The Bible Knowledge Commentary: An Exposition of the Scriptures*, ed. J.F. Walvoord and R.B. Zuck (Wheaton, IL: Victor, 1983-c. 1985).

[3] Dr. Willard F. Harley Jr., *His Needs, Her Needs* (Old Tappan, NJ: Fleming H. Revell, 1986), pp. 106, 108.

# About the Authors

*Gil Stieglitz* is an internationally recognized author, speaker, catalyst, counselor, professor, and leadership consultant. He is Executive Pastor of Adventure Christian Church, a mega-church of 4,000 in Roseville, California. He teaches at Christian Universities and graduate schools in practical theology (Biola, William Jessup, Western Seminary). He is the President of Principles to Live By, an organization committed to teaching God's principles in a life-giving way. He sits on several boards, including Thriving Churches International, a ministry extension of Bayside Church, and Courage Worldwide, an organization that builds homes throughout the world to rescue children forced into sexual slavery. He has been a denominational executive for fifteen years with the Evangelical Free Church of America and was the senior pastor of a vibrant church in southern California for seventeen years. He is proud of the work done in his counseling ministry over the past thirty years, where he has spent thousands of hours helping couples with their marriages. It is his life's work, as well as his intellectual understanding of the Scriptures, that Dr. Stieglitz draws upon for the writing and teaching of *God's Radical Plan for Wives, God's Radical Plan for Husbands,* and *Marital Intelligence.* Learn more about Gil at www.gilstieglitz.com.

*Dana Stieglitz* has been wife to Gil for twenty-five years, and is the mother of three beautiful girls. She is a nurse practitioner with a Bachelor's and Master's degree in nursing, and is finishing her

Doctorate in Nursing in 2014. She is a certified Stott Pilates Instructor and works at Kaiser Hospital in Roseville and Sacramento. Dana co-authored *God's Radical Plan for Wives* with her husband, offering her wisdom and insight into the work.

*Jennifer Edwards* is an author and Bible teacher whose passion is helping women to understand the truth of God's Word and how it applies to their lives in practical ways. She firmly believes there is both power and peace when a woman embraces God's prescribed role of wife in a marriage, which led to the writing of *God's Radical Plan for Wives Companion Bible Study Workbook.* Jennifer is a graduate student at Western Seminary, where she is earning a Master's degree in Biblical Studies and Theology. With her no-nonsense and transparent approach, she is a popular speaker and teacher, encouraging women to adopt *God's Radical Plan for Wives* using the principles highlighted in this book. She is an established editor and freelance writer, serving Christian authors and publishers. Jennifer and her husband, Mike, have been married for twenty-two years. Together, they are raising two teenagers in Loomis, California. You can learn more about Jennifer at www.jenniferedwards.net.

# Useful Resources for Marriage
## By Gil Stieglitz

*God's Radical Plan for Wives Companion Bible Study,* by Jennifer Edwards. Nine lessons over ten weeks, perfect for individual or small group use.

*God's Radical Plan for Husbands: Really Loving Your Wife*

*Marital Intelligence: A Foolproof Guide for Saving and Strengthening Marriage*

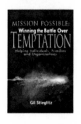

*Mission Possible: Winning the Battle Over Temptation*

*A complete list of resources is available at www.ptlb.com.*

# Other Resources

## By Gil Stieglitz

Available in various formats, from books to e-books, to Kindle, audio & podcasts. Check out www.ptlb.com.

*Becoming Courageous*

*Breaking Satanic Bondage*

*Deep Happiness: The 8 Secrets*

*Developing A Christian Worldview*

*Going Deep In Prayer: 40 Days of In-Depth Prayer*

*Leading a Thriving Ministry: 10 Indispensable Leadership Skills*

*Spiritual Disciplines of a C.H.R.I.S.T.I.A.N.*

*Intensive Training in Christian Spirituality*

*They Laughed When I Wrote Another Book About Prayer, Then They Read It: How To Make Prayer Work*

*Touching the Face of God: 40 Days of Adoring God*

*Why There Has to Be a Hell*

*Becoming A Godly Parent*

*Biblical Meditation: The Keys To Transformation*

*Everyday Spiritual Warfare*

*God's Guide To Handling Money*

*The 4 Keys to a Great Family*

*The Ten Commandments*

If you would be interested in having Dr. Gil Stieglitz

Come to speak to your group, you can contact him through the

Principles To Live By website:

**www.ptlb.com**

**www.gilstieglitz.com**

CPSIA information can be obtained
at www.ICGtesting.com
Printed in the USA
LVOW11s1131270717
542802LV00001B/117/P